O
INDIA SHORT
INTRODUCTIONS

THE CIVIL SERVICES
IN INDIA

The Oxford India Short
Introductions are concise,
stimulating, and accessible guides
to different aspects of India.
Combining authoritative analysis,
new ideas, and diverse perspectives,
they discuss subjects which are
topical yet enduring, as also
emerging areas of study and debate.

OTHER TITLES IN THE SERIES

OXFORD
INDIA SHORT
INTRODUCTIONS

THE CIVIL SERVICES IN INDIA

S.K. DAS

OXFORD
UNIVERSITY PRESS

OXFORD
UNIVERSITY PRESS

Oxford University Press is a department of the University of Oxford.
It furthers the University's objective of excellence in research, scholarship,
and education by publishing worldwide. Oxford is a registered trademark of
Oxford University Press in the UK and in certain other countries

Published in India by
Oxford University Press
YMCA Library Building, 1 Jai Singh Road, New Delhi 110001, India

ISBN-13: 978-0-19-808609-3
ISBN-10: 0-19-808609-1

Typeset in 11/15.6 Bembo Std
by Excellent Laser Typesetters, Pitampura, Delhi 110 034
Printed in India at G.H. Prints Pvt Ltd, New Delhi 110 020

Contents

Introduction

The civil service system has always formed the backbone of administration in any country, irrespective of whether its government is headed by a king, president, prime minister, governor, or chief minister. In common parlance, the terms 'civil service' and 'bureaucracy' are often used interchangeably. It will be useful here to understand what these terms mean.

The original use of the term 'bureaucracy' referred to a cloth that covered the desks of eighteenth-century French officials. It was a way of describing a government ruled by officials. Over time, the term 'bureaucracy' acquired a negative connotation. It was used to describe procedures which were unreasonably time-consuming, and led to the harassment of people and petty tyranny of officials.

On account of this bad association, the term 'civil servant' came to be used instead. There is very little difference between a bureaucrat and a civil servant, although the latter also means a full-time employee of the government. The term 'civil service', as it is used now, has two distinct meanings. First, it is a branch of the governmental service in which individuals are employed on the basis of merit as tested in an examination. Second, it refers to a body of employees in any governmental agency other than the military and the judiciary.

The origins of civil services go back a long way. It was civil services that formed the key to the great river valley civilizations that flourished as early as 3,000 BC. The water sources of the Nile, the Tigris and Euphrates, the Indus, and the Yellow rivers formed the lifeblood of the civilizations they nurtured. There was, thus, a need to regulate these resources. It required officials to monitor the river flow and supervise their distribution into irrigation systems.

These officials were the first civil servants. They also took part in construction activities, which were organized along military lines. Once in place, it was only a matter of time before these officials took over the administration of the entire state.

In China the civil service system has been in place since, at least, 200 BC, and has played a crucial role in the preservation of the empire. Civil servants were recruited on the basis of merit and serving the state was considered a great privilege in China. Similarly in Japan, the system has existed since AD 645. This is despite the fact that there were frequent changes in the ruling dynasties in Japan.

We also have examples of powerful empires that crumbled because of the absence of civil services. The African empires, for instance, lasted only for brief periods of time because they lacked a proper system. Similarly, the Carolingian Empire came under strain once its civil service disintegrated.

The idea of a modern state, in its present form, developed in Europe in the Middle Ages. It involved a lot of nation-building activities in Europe at that time. Developing an efficient civil service was essential to such processes; the early leaders being France, Prussia, and England.

Interestingly, in these European countries, civil servants were not appointed on the basis of merit. In

England, for example, until the early nineteenth century, the appointment of civil servants depended on the pleasure of those in power. There was no common system of remuneration; and corruption was rampant. The government offices were seen as private property, which, like any other asset, could be sold or used for making money.

The reforms in civil services were introduced in these European countries during the nineteenth century when industrialization was taken up in a big way. Such countries, therefore, could not afford a corrupt administration. So they started restructuring the existing system in which officials would be appointed on the basis of merit and given a lifelong career. In order to curb corruption, systems were established to ensure uniform application of law, rules, and regulations.

These reforms yielded impressive gains. They not only succeeded in establishing merit-based systems but also checked corruption. However, they ended up creating a rigid and rule-bound civil service. By insisting on a strict application of law, rules, and regulations, the reforms certainly prevented civil servants from misappropriating funds but inadvertently made it difficult for the officials to manage public money in a meaningful manner.

It was true that these reforms restricted arbitrary dismissals of civil servants, but they also made sure that no one, not even the most incompetent official, could be removed. Thus, in their obsession with how things should be done in accordance with rules and regulations, the reforms ended up ensuring that civil servants do not deliver results. As a result, the system that finally emerged out of the nineteenth-century reforms was slow, inefficient, and rule-bound.

For most part of the late nineteenth and twentieth centuries, the tasks that civil servants were called upon to perform were simple and repetitive in nature. Most people wanted similar kind of services and were not critical about the quality rendered. This meant that the civil service constructed roads, railways, and schools; built parks, jails, and libraries; maintained law and order; and generally upheld the authority of the state. The system, therefore, functioned in an environment where change, if any, took place slowly and gradually, and people had similar wants and needs.

It was only by the 1970s and 1980s that the functioning of civil services came under intense scrutiny.

By this time, the size of the services had grown enormously and the wage bills were high. Civil services had also, by then, come to acquire too many people and too many grades. The range of services that officials provided was as diverse as their grades. Civil servants guarded art treasures in museums and convicts in prisons; they minted coins and made maps; they collected taxes and gave away benefits; and they prevented smuggling and made weather predictions. But the quality of all these services left a lot to be desired.

It was at about this time that questions began to be raised as to whether the prevailing system was of any use to citizens who wanted better and faster services. It was also pointed out that the civil service had become too rigid and rule-bound, and was steeped in bureaucratic behaviour. Bureaucratic behaviour is a term often used to denote the painfully slow and ponderous conduct which is all about the unrelenting routine and endless procedures, and does not respond to the needs of the people being governed. These traits led to the frustration and harassment of citizens at the hands of the civil servants.

It was only natural, then, that citizens were disenchanted with the civil service. They believed they deserved a better system: one that delivers services to make them healthier, more secure, and better equipped to tackle the challenges that they face; one that responds directly to their basic needs, such as education and healthcare, and which acts for the society as a whole; one which is available when they need it, and provides for services to improve the quality of their lives; and one which is focused on results rather than rules and regulations.

It was, therefore, time for another round of reforms in civil services, in the 1990s. These are currently taking place in civil service systems across the globe. Particularly important are the ones being brought about in countries like the United Kingdom, Australia, and New Zealand, with whom India shares a common ancestry of civil service traditions. They focus on the benefits that people should derive from the usage of government funds. They emphasize the importance of measuring results that have been achieved and have led to enhancing the quality of life of the citizens. While some countries have already reformed their civil services along these lines, in some others it is still an ongoing process.

This short introduction is a very brief history of civil services during the last 5,000 years. It is against this backdrop that we analyse the civil service system in India: its evolution, role, structure, and size; the methods of recruitment and training; performance management systems and mechanisms of accountability; and finally, the relationship between civil servants and their political masters.

1

Evolution of Civil Services in India

The legends of the Aryans speak of how administrative arrangements evolved in ancient India. The
gods, at war with demons, were on the verge of
defeat. In desperation, they got together and elected
a king to lead them. The origins of the early Aryan
administrative system may perhaps be traced to these
legends.

An administrative system evolved with the king
as the focal point. A court of elders assisted the king,
but his principal advisers were the commander of
the troops and the chief priest who also doubled as
an astrologer. Spies, messengers, and a superintendent
of dicing completed the king's civil service. These
kingdoms were small in size and the administrative

organization resembled a family set-up of which the king was the head.

The Mauryas

When the Aryans settled down in the Gangetic region, there were a number of kingdoms. The battle for supremacy among these kingdoms lasted for about a hundred years, but finally Magadha emerged victorious and established the Mauryan Empire. The emperor was at the top of the Mauryan administrative structure which consisted of *mantrin*s and the *amatya*s. While the mantrins were the highest advisers to the emperor, the amatyas were the civil servants. There were three kinds of amatyas: the highest, intermediate, and the lowest, based on their qualifications.

There were two key civil servants: the s*amahartr* and s*amnidhatr*. The samahartr prepared the annual budget, kept accounts, and fixed the revenue to be collected. It was his job to ensure that the expenditure did not exceed the revenues. The samnidhatr, assisted by a number of civil servants, kept record of the taxes that came in from various parts of the empire. He was in charge of the stores, and of the actual revenue and other income received by the government. Everything that needed to be stored and guarded was the responsibility of the samnidhatr.

There were many major departments of the government, each headed by a senior civil servant. *Panyadhyaksha*, the superintendent of trade, headed the commercial department dealing with internal and external trade. *Sitadhyaksha*, the superintendent of agriculture, looked after the state farms, government lands, and regulation of land belonging to individuals. *Rathadhyaksha*, the superintendent of chariots, was the head of the defence department. *Swarnadhyaksha*, the superintendent of mines, looked after the mining of various minerals such as gold, copper, iron, and diamonds. *Vanyadhyaksha*, the superintendent of forests, was the head of the department of forestry. *Bharadhyaksha*, the superintendent of weights, was the head of the weights and measures department. *Sutradhyaksha*, the superintendent of textiles, was in charge of textile factories.

The kingdom was divided into four divisions, each under a civil servant called the *sthanika*. Under the sthanika, there were junior civil servants called *gopas*, each in charge of five or ten villages. Next in line was the village headman, called the *gramika*. He was also a civil servant, with the power to send people to prison. It was the duty of these civil servants to maintain records of all agricultural and other holdings in the villages under their charge, and take a census of the households, record the number of inhabitants, with full details of their profession, properties, income, expenditure, and the revenue received from each village. With such information, the samahartr maintained a record of all towns and villages in the empire, classifying them as big, middling, and small, and providing information about their wealth in grains, cattle, and money.

Administration of Pataliputra, the capital of the empire, was the responsibility of the *paur*, the chief of the town. The paur had thirty civil servants under him, divided into six committees of five each. Each committee supervised one of these functions: industry and arts, welfare of foreigners, registration of birth and death, trade and commerce, public sale of manufactured goods, and collection of tax on articles sold. The paur also maintained law and order and general cleanliness of the city.

The qualifications necessary in order to be appointed as a civil servant were: loyalty and integrity. The tests prescribed for the purpose (*dharmopadha, arthopadha, bhayopadha,* and *kamopadha*) were to essentially test these qualities of the person. Corruption or embezzlement by the civil servant invited severe penalties. The corrupt civil servant was smeared with cow dung and ashes. His head was shaved and he was showered with brickbats. His offence was proclaimed throughout the town or village. In more serious cases of corruption, the punishment was death, and the death was caused by official torture.

The Mauryan administration had a system of secret agents whose services were used for checking on the honesty of civil servants. There were two types of secret agents: the *samstha* who was stationed in a single place, and the *sanchara,* who moved from place to place. These secret agents disguised themselves as monks and collected intelligence about whether the civil servants were honest or dishonest.

On the whole, during the time of the Mauryan Empire, there was an elaborate system of civil service and an array of offices, stretching from villages to the central departments manned by civil servants with specific duties and responsibilities.

Delhi Sultanate

After the Mauyran Empire disintegrated, administration was in a state of constant change for a period of 1,500 years. A number of rulers came, ruled and sank without leaving behind any memorable administrative system. The Delhi Sultanate (1200–1526) was an exception. It was able to establish a recognizable administrative structure.

The Sultanate was a conquest state, and therefore, it became necessary for the rulers to establish their control over newly-conquered territories. The ruler appointed his followers as civil servants and put them in charge of these territories. But it was important, at the same time, to ensure that they were kept under the ruler's control.

The strategy was to grant land to the followers on a temporary basis and to transfer the holders of these land grants as frequently as possible so as to exercise control over them. The land grants were made with certain conditions. First, the civil servant was to pay a part of the revenue from the land to the ruler. Second, he had to maintain a specified number of troops for the ruler to be deployed at the time of war. During the time of peace, the ruler reviewed the collection of revenue, the state of administration, and the mobilization of troops.

The Sultanate pattern of granting land to civil servants as compensation for services rendered in lieu of cash salaries was known as the *iqta* system. The Sultan had his own land which was meant for his personal needs and looked after directly by his retainers. Civil servants who were granted land, collected revenue from the areas they were put in charge of. They also performed administrative functions such as maintaining peace and imposing order. In addition, they discharged judicial functions such as settling disputes. The civil servants in the Sultanate thus came to exercise political, judicial, and administrative powers.

Over time, the *iqtadars* started treating their iqtas as hereditary. Ala-ud-din Khilji made some changes in the iqta system to ensure that the iqtas were not made hereditary by the iqtadars. He cancelled all grants made by the previous Sultans and made fresh grants. But Firuz Shah Tugluq, one of the later rulers of the sultanate, returned all these lands to their previous holders.

In the process, it came to be recognized that the iqta system had become hereditary.

The iqtadars of the Delhi Sultanate had begun their career from being personal servants of the Sultan. In course of time when the iqtas became hereditary, the iqtadars invented elaborate genealogies to establish their aristocratic origins. The ample income from the iqtas enabled the civil servants to maintain a lifestyle of great luxury.

The head of the civil administration in the Delhi Sultanate was the *wazir*, who supervised collection of revenue, checking of accounts, and regulation of expenditure. There were three other senior civil servants—one was the head of military, the second was the head of interstate relations, and the third, the chancellor, who was in charge of spies stationed throughout the Sultanate reporting on the administration of the iqtadars.

On the whole, civil servants in the Delhi Sultanate were selected on the basis of their loyalty to the ruler and were given land grants for rendering their services. Unlike the Mauryan civil service, there was no system of offices and the civil servants held positions that were loosely defined.

The Mughals

The Mughal rulers, like those in the Delhi Sultanate, appointed their followers as civil servants by giving them land grants, but they were able to keep their followers under control by keeping these land grants on a temporary basis and by transferring the civil servants from one place to another very frequently. The Mughal civil service was based on the *mansabdari* system. Every *mansabdar* was given a *mansab* (a rank or command), which determined his position in the civil service.

The mansabdari system was graded across thirty-three categories of command, ranging from a commander of ten to a commander of 5,000. A *panch-hazari* or the commander of 5,000 was a top civil servant. The mansabdari system was essentially a pool of civil servants available for civil or military deployment.

There was also a system of assignment of land revenue to civil servants in lieu of the payment of salary. This was the *jagirdari* system. Under this system, the civil servant, after presenting his troops for inspection, was given a *jagir*. By the seventeenth century, the jagir system had become the accepted way for the ruler to reward the loyalty of his civil servants.

The administrative structure consisted of seven categories of civil servants. The *sipah salar*, the commander of the army, was a mansabdar who controlled the largest body of troops in the area. He was in charge of the provincial affairs and was responsible for maintaining peace and order. The *faujdar*, a subordinate of the sipah salar, commanded the largest body of cavalry, and was in charge of controlling the cultivators and monitoring the performance of local revenue collectors and jagirdars. The *quazi*s were responsible for administration of justice. The *kotwal*, the chief officer in the urban areas, maintained order in the cities. The *amal-guzar* was the chief financial officer at the sub-provincial level, in charge of collection of revenue.

The Mughal rulers controlled their civil servants in several ways. The rulers travelled widely and frequently so that they could keep a watch over their civil servants. Of their 200 years of rule, the Mughal rulers spent almost 40 per cent of their time on tour. Civil servants, on their part, were expected to attend the imperial court regularly. Mansabdars were required to visit the imperial court on a number of occasions—after each change in office, after a change in jagir posting, on being promoted, and on most days of special celebration. For mansabdars, advancement in their career depended as much on putting in regular appearances at the imperial court as on the quality and value of gifts they presented to the Mughal rulers.

Another means of control was the frequent transfer of civil servants. No civil servant was allowed to keep his jagir or stay at his post for more than three or four years. There were also spies stationed in cities and towns throughout the empire. These spies were responsible for keeping the emperor informed of the doings of the mansabdars.

But the most important method of control was to keep the possession of the jagir as temporary as possible. The jagir was given to the mansabdar for only so long as he held office and was taken away by the emperor on his death. Even as the mansabdar was on his deathbed, it was the usual practice to put the royal seal on his coffers and beat the servants to get the details of the property of the dying mansabdar.

Since the jagir was only for the lifetime of the mansabdar, he used to indulge in all kinds of extravagances while the mansab lasted. Surrounded by huge hordes of retainers who pandered to the whims and fancies of their masters, the mansabdars used to enjoy themselves by building beautiful palaces, laying intricate gardens, and constructing domed tombs. Such lavish lifestyles required that the mansabdars make as much money as possible. So, they exploited the people over whom they ruled, and were in the habit of helping themselves to whatever they could lay their hands on.

On the whole, the strategy of the Mughal rulers to control their civil servants by keeping the assignment of jagirs temporary was successful. But it had serious social and economic consequences. It led to unlimited exploitation of the people.

British India

By 1765, the term 'civil servant' started appearing in the records of the East India Company to describe its officials. This was done to distinguish between those engaged in civil and military activities. Before 1765, the lowest functionary of the East India Company was called a 'factor', meaning a commercial agent. The trading station where the factors worked was called a 'factory', and the place where a number of factories were grouped together was called a 'settlement'.

In 1765, the Company ordered for only writers (clerks appointed by the company) to be recruited, and the point of entry to the civil service of the East India Company became that of the writer. Appointment as a writer was only by nomination. To be appointed as a writer, it was necessary to get a nomination from a director of the East India Company. Nominations were made only on financial considerations. The directors made a lot of money out of these nominations. The position of a writer commanded high prices. A newspaper article in 1772 reported that posts of writers had been sold for 2,000 to 3,000 pounds each, and in 1783, there was an advertisement in a newspaper offering 1,000 guineas for a writer's place in Bengal.

Almost all the young people who joined the civil service of the Company, came to India with the single objective of amassing a fortune as quickly as possible. India was considered a gold mine, sizable fortunes were made, and corruption became a way of life. It was customary in colonial India to offer money or expensive gifts to civil servants to get favourable orders. On the whole, the rule of the East India Company was one of sheer plunder by its officials. It became such a big scandal in England that the British Parliament had to step in and pass the Charter Act of 1793, which required the directors of the Company to take an oath that they will not make any nomination in exchange for gifts and money.

Finally, the Act of 1833 ordered that, for every vacancy in the Company's civil service, at least four candidates be nominated by the directors, and the best one among them be selected by a written entrance examination. The Act also provided that candidates appearing for the entrance examination should belong to the age group of seventeen to twenty. As a result, very few civil servants had the benefit of a university education; almost all the writers who came to India were very young and only had school education.

Macaulay Committee

Merit became the only basis for selection when the appointment to civil services of the East India Company was thrown open to competition by an Act of Parliament in 1853. This was also the time when the Charter of the East India Company was being renewed for the last time. The Act, however, allowed the directors of the Company to make nominations till April 1854. When the Act of 1853 was passed, a committee was appointed, with Lord Macaulay as the Chairman, to advise on the subjects for the examination for recruiting candidates for the civil service.

The committee submitted its report in 1854. The committee's recommendations covered three important aspects. The first was about the age of the candidates. The committee recommended a minimum age of eighteen and a maximum age of twenty-three. This was because they desired that candidates for the examination should have had college education, preferably with a good degree from some of the best universities in England. In the words of the committee,

> We think it desirable that a considerable number of the civil servants of the Company should be men who have taken their first degree in arts at Oxford and Cambridge. At present the line is drawn as if it had been expressly meant to exclude the bachelors of these universities.

The second related to the subjects for the examination, with the recommended ones being English language and literature, history, mathematics, natural sciences, moral and political philosophy, Sanskrit, and Arabic.

The Committee's third recommendation was that successful candidates should be trained for a number of years before they assumed duties. It recommended a training programme during which the civil service trainees were required to study four subjects: Indian history and geography, law, finance, and one Indian language. At the end of the training period, they had to take a second examination. While the position in the first examination entitled them to a choice of their provinces, the position in the second examination gave them their rank in the civil service.

The merit-based system put in place in the 1850s by implementing the recommendations of the Macaulay Committee continues to the present day.

Officers of the Indian Civil Service

After 1855, appointment to the Indian Civil Service (ICS) came to be totally based on merit. Of those who entered the ICS, more than two-thirds were university men, and more than one-third were graduates.

Out of the several universities in England, the Oxford University supplied by far the largest number of candidates and Cambridge came next. Therefore, the ICS was an elite service which could afford to pick and choose its members. It was said only with a slight hint of exaggeration that nobody without a first-class honours degree stood a chance.

The ICS was a small and compact service. At no point of time did it exceed a number a little more than a thousand. Even at its peak, there were only 1,032 officers in 1931. The ICS numbers accounted for only 0.001 per cent of all the government servants in British India, the strength of the latter in 1931 alone being one million for the total Indian population of 353 million.

Although the ICS was smaller in size, its officers occupied all the important positions in the administration. These positions were reserved for them in the districts and in secretariats, both at the provincial and central levels. This system was crucial to maintaining the imperial interests of the British in India.

About 50 per cent of the ICS officers worked at the district level. In colonial India these districts formed the basic units of administration. The officer in charge of a district was known by various designations such

17

as the District Magistrate (because of his magisterial duties), the Collector (because he collected government revenues), the District Officer (because he was the chief coordinator in the district), and the Deputy Commissioner (in the backward areas). The officer exercised a large number of powers as the head of the revenue collection agency, the law and order agency, the magistracy, and local authorities.

Roughly 25 per cent of the ICS officers were stationed at the headquarters of the provinces. They worked as secretaries to the government, and also as heads of important field departments like agriculture, excise, posts and telegraphs, and public instructions, and even occupied the post of the Inspector General of Police. The framework of the provincial government was so designed that only a few ICS officers in the headquarters of each province were able to exercise control over the functioning of the government.

About 10 per cent of the ICS officers worked for the Government of India in the secretariat, either at the centre or in the provinces. The officers handled questions of policy in a manner that would promote the economic and political interests of the imperial government.

The ICS officers were known for their honesty and integrity; and bribery and corruption were unheard of. The ICS, in the course of its long rule of the country spread over 160 years, had established a great reputation for itself as an incorruptible organ of the government. All officers were guided by the *Phal–Phul* rule which meant that they were forbidden to accept gifts other than fruits and flowers.

One thing that helped was that an ICS officer acquired a respectable income. On joining the ICS and still in their early twenties, the officers made around 300 pounds a year—twice as much as the stipend of an average clergyman in England. As the Collector of a district and still in his thirties, an ICS officer earned between 1,600 and 2,400 pounds a year. In his fifties, an ICS officer earned about 3,600 pounds a year— comfortably exceeding what a senior judge earned in England. In any case, all ICS officers retired to the same pension of 1,000 pounds a year. An ICS officer, as a prospective husband, mothers told their daughters, was worth 1,000 pounds a year, dead or alive.

The popular image of the civil servant was one of a courageous, self-confident officer who had an aura of command: an officer doing his duty in a remote rural district, and a person capable of remarkable self-discipline and hard work. The ICS officers had an intellectual aura and supposedly knew everything that there was to know. That was why an ICS officer was called the *sab-jaanta* ICS by the people.

But, above all, the image of the ICS, particularly that of the district officer, was based on the *mai-baap* principle. They were considered the mai-baaps, the mothers and fathers of the people. They spent all day and most of the night riding around their districts: punishing crimes, collecting revenue, resolving disputes, relieving scarcity, and digging canals. They had no families to distract them, no belongings to slow them down, no weaknesses of any kind, and heat or sun or rain mattered not to them. It was only natural then, that for the average, respectful Indian, the ICS officers were truly heaven-born.

It is true that most of the people who worked for the colonial government in India were Indians. Although many civil servants were needed to govern a subcontinent the size of Europe containing about one-fifth of the world's population, pre-eminent among the civil servants were the officers of the ICS. The ICS officers were clearly the leaders in the civil service and they decided the basic framework of the administration.

Civil Service in Independent India

When India became independent, many things changed, but the basic framework of the civil service continued. The ICS was succeeded by the Indian Administrative Service (IAS). When recruitment to the ICS stopped in the 1940s, recruitment to the IAS began. Over the years, IAS officers gradually moved in as the ICS personnel made their exits. Although changes in the range of posts held by the IAS and the nature of their work reflected a changed orientation of the Indian state, the location and activities of officers broadly followed the same pattern as in the colonial government.

In the normal course, there would have been nothing strange about such continuity because civil servants do not take kindly to any change. But this was different.

During the independence movement, the ICS was seen as the instrument of the imperial power and the Congress Party had all along declared that they would

21

abolish the ICS and all that it stood for. That did not happen. In 1964, Pandit Jawaharlal Nehru was asked what he considered to be his greatest failure as India's Prime Minister. He said, 'I could not change the administration, it is still a colonial administration'.

2

Size and Structure

It is the government that provides the framework for the size and structure of the civil services. This framework determines not only the total number and levels of civil servants, but also the context in which they carry out their functions. The structure provides the system of coordination between the divisions, sub-divisions, and other units of the government, and also the channels of communication with other agencies and members of the public.

Size

When we talk about the size of civil services in India, it is necessary to define the personnel who constitute it. While compiling government statistics, the categories included are employees of the Central and state governments, employees of quasi-government organizations such as public sector undertakings and nationalized banks, and the local bodies. It excludes the judiciary and members of the armed forces.

According to government statistics, the total number of civil servants in India in 2007 was 17.99 million, or say, 18 million. Out of this, the number of Central government employees was 2.80 million while that of the state governments' was 7.21 million. The number of employees of quasi-government bodies, both in the Central and state governments, was 5.85 million and the same in local bodies was 2.13 million.

How does the number of civil servants compare with the number of people employed in the private sector? The total number of people employed in the private sector in India in 2007 was 9.28 million. Therefore, at a rough estimate, it can be concluded that the number of civil servants in the country is almost double the number of people employed in the private sector.

Do we have too many civil servants? One useful benchmark would be to compare with the previous years. As we have seen, in 1931, the total number of people working in the government was 1 million. In

24

1953, the number had become 4 million. It has gone up steadily after that. The number was almost 8 million in 1963, 12 million in 1973, 16.5 million in 1983, and 19.3 million in 1993. It peaked at 19.58 million in 1997.

What led to such a significant rise? It was because, after the country became independent, the number of tasks a civil servant was expected to perform increased substantially. In independent India, the changed circumstances called for the priorities of the government to be changed. Civil servants were now required to carry out tasks which were developmental in nature. This was in addition to the regulatory tasks they traditionally carried out. In response to changing circumstances and priorities, new ministries and departments were created. This called for a larger number of civil servants to implement the developmental agenda. Thus, the number of civil servants went up by a factor of four, between 1953 and 1997.

The expansion in the civil service made the government wage bill unsustainably large. By the 1990s, the wage bill of the civil services had become the single largest item of government expenditure. In 1997–8, the Government of India (GoI) spent about Rs 15,000 crore on the pay and perquisites of civil servants. In other words, this would translate to about 1.5 per cent of the country's gross domestic product (GDP). The state governments too, spend an equal amount on the pay and perquisites of their civil servants. So, 3 per cent of GDP is spent on the upkeep of the civil service in the country. This is, indeed, a very large sum.

The Fifth Pay Commission recommended that the number of civil servants be cut down to one-third of its current strength. As a result, the governments initiated several measures to this end. These included a ban on employment, not filling up vacancies, and enforcing strict economy in the expenditure incurred by the civil services. This resulted in the numbers coming down appreciably. From the peak number of 19.58 million in 1997, it came down to about 18 million in 2007.

The Sixth Pay Commission did not make any specific recommendation about the number of civil servants. Therefore, it led to no appreciable reduction after 2007. For the year 2009, the number stood at 17.79 million while for the year 2010, it was 17.86 million.

Structure

An important feature of the civil service system in India is its classification based on the concept of 'service'.

Under this concept, civil service posts are grouped into distinct homogenous cadres under a common service named on the basis of specific functions attached to these posts. The various categories of the services at the Central and the state levels have been classified in two ways.

First, they are categorized into three broad groups: the Central Services, the All India Services, and the state civil services. The Central Services function under GoI. The All India Services are common to the Central government and the state governments. State civil services function only under the state governments.

Second, the Central Services and the state civil services are classified into Groups A, B, C, and D, based on their roles, ranks, and responsibilities.

Central Services

These services administer subjects that are assigned to the Union Government in the Constitution of India. These are subjects like Posts and Telegraphs, Railways, Customs and Central Excise, Income Tax, Telecommunications, and so on. Central Services can be further categorized into (a) non-technical services,

(b) technical services, (c) health services, (d) railway services, (e) para-defence services, and (f) central secretariat services.

NON-TECHNICAL SERVICES

These are meant to administer non-technical areas of administration in the Indian government as per the items listed in the distribution of responsibilities laid down in the Constitution. They consist of the Indian Audit and Accounts Service, Indian Postal Service, Indian Revenue Service, Indian Customs and Central Excise Service, Central Information Service, Indian Economic Service, Indian Civil Accounts Service, Central Company Law Service, Central Labour Service, Indian Legal Service, Indian Supply Service, Indian Inspection Service, and Central Trade Service.

TECHNICAL SERVICES

Technical Services, including the engineering services, perform on the technical side in the Government of India. They consist of the Central Power Engineering Service, Central Architects' Service, Central Electrical

28

and Mechanical Engineering Service, Central Engineering Service, Central Water Engineering Service, Indian Meteorological Service, Survey of India, Geological Survey of India, Central Engineering Service (Roads), and Border Roads Engineering Service.

HEALTH SERVICES

The Health Services work in the area of health and consist of the Central Health Service (General Duty Cadre).

RAILWAY SERVICES

These services working in the Department of Railways include the Indian Railway Service of Engineers, Indian Railway Service of Mechanical Engineers, Indian Railway Service of Signal Engineers, Indian Railway Service of Electrical Engineers, Indian Railway Stores Service, Indian Railway Traffic Service, Indian Railway Personnel Service, Indian Railways Accounts Service, Indian Railway Medical Service, and Indian Railway Protection Force.

PARA-DEFENCE SERVICES

These services come under the control of the Ministry of Defence. They consist of the Defence Aeronautical Quality Assurance Service, Defence Quality Assurance Service, Indian Naval Armament Service, Defence Research and Development Service, Indian Ordnance Factory Service, Indian Ordnance Factory Health Service, Indian Defence Estate Service, Indian Defence Accounts Service, Military Engineering Service (Civilian Component), and Armed Forces Headquarters Civil Service.

CENTRAL SECRETARIAT SERVICE

Civil servants in the Central Secretariat Service provide the permanent set-up in the secretariat of the Central Government. The Central Secretariat consists of civil servants such as Directors, Deputy Secretaries, Under Secretaries, and Section Officers, as well as stenographers and the clerical cadre. The Central Secretariat Service provides a strong framework for the Secretariat of GoI, as well as a delivery system for making policy and a monitoring and review system for implementation of policy.

All India Services

The Constitution of India provides for the creation of All India Services. As mentioned earlier, these are common to both the Central and the state governments. There are three such services, namely, the Indian Administrative Service, the Indian Police Service, and the Indian Forest Service. The Indian Constitution had originally mentioned only two services belonging to the All India Services, namely the Indian Administrative Service and the Indian Police Service. Subsequently, the Indian Forest Service was constituted as an All India Service. The Constitution also mentions an All India Judicial Service, which has not yet been formed.

INDIAN ADMINISTRATIVE SERVICE

The Indian Administrative Service (IAS) is the successor to the Indian Civil Service (ICS), the legendary

31

'steel frame' of the British Raj. It is the most important among all the services in the country. This importance is derived partly from the advantage that the IAS enjoys over other civil services in pay scales and faster promotions, and partly from the job content of the positions that IAS officers hold.

The IAS is a mandarin type of service similar to that in Britain, France, and Japan. What this means is that the officials are selected on the basis of an open competitive examination. But, where the IAS differs from the civil services in Britain, France, or Japan is in the mobility of the officers in the administrative system. They not only work at various levels of government—in Central government, state governments, local bodies, and public sector undertakings—but also move across ministries and functions to a much larger extent than in most other mandarin civil service systems.

The IAS officers, on their appointment, are allotted to a particular state. It is in this state that they specialize and learn the language of the state, customs, laws, and so on, and pass examinations in these subjects. All their postings in the field such as in the subdivision, district, etc., are in this state. Part of their career is usually spent in the Central Government.

Key positions in the state governments are reserved for IAS officers. These positions are called cadre posts. What this means is that these posts can be held only by IAS officers. This is a deliberate feature of the All India Service system intended to promote quality, impartiality, integrity, and an all-India outlook. Thus the secretaries in charge of departments in all state governments and the Chief Secretary (the head of the civil service in the state government) are always IAS officers.

INDIAN POLICE SERVICE

The Indian Police Service (IPS) succeeded the Indian Police (IP) which constituted the top police service in British India. Like the IAS, the IPS is a mandarin civil service in the sense that its officers are recruited through an open, competitive examination.

IPS officers, on their appointment to the service, are allotted to a state cadre. It is in this state that the officers specialize and learn the local language. Most of their careers are spent in states where they undertake field postings like in subdivisions, districts, ranges, and apex organizations in the state governments. IPS officers are also sent on deputation to the Central Government where they work in prestigious national police organizations.

In the state government, key police positions are declared as cadre posts, signifying that these posts can be held only by IPS officers. For example, the senior-most police assignments like the Inspector General of Police and the Director-General of Police (the head of the state police department) are designated as cadre posts of the IPS.

INDIAN FOREST SERVICE

The Indian Forest Service (IFoS) was the only All India Service to be created in independent India. Like in the IAS and the IPS, the officers of the IFoS are selected through an open, competitive examination held on an all-India basis.

The career pattern of the IFoS officers is very similar to those in the IAS and the IPS. They are allotted to a particular state cadre where they specialize and learn the local language. They start their careers in the forest divisions and are promoted progressively to higher responsibilities in the state forest departments.

Some forest officers are sent on deputation to work in prestigious national forest organizations.

Certain important posts in the forest department are designated as cadre posts which only officers of the IFoS can occupy. Such cadre posts typically include the Chief Conservator of Forests and the Principal Chief Conservator of Forests (the head of the state forest department).

State Civil Services

The state civil services function only under the state governments. They include various services which perform different administrative functions of their governments. These services administer subjects allocated to the states in the Constitution; implement laws made by the state legislatures, and on occasion, certain central laws where they are so authorized. The officers of the state civil services have their duties confined to the territories of their respective states.

Some of the state civil service officers are promoted to All India Services like the IAS, IPS, and IFS. According to the present system, one-third of the All India Services are filled by promotion from the state civil services. It takes about eight to twenty-five years for the state civil service officers to get promoted to the All India Services, but there is wide variation across states.

Group A, B, C, and D Categories

The civil service, both in the Government of India and the state governments, is categorized into four groups: Group A (which includes the All India Services and the Central Services), Group B, Group C, and Group D. This classification is based broadly on the rank, status, and degree of responsibility attached to posts.

This classification is as in a hierarchy. The posts belonging to Group A carry higher responsibilities and include senior management positions in the ministries and departments as well as in field organizations. Civil servants at the junior level in Group A and the staff in Group B are the middle level of the government. Civil servants in Group C perform supervisory functions and carry out routine tasks while some of them give clerical assistance. Staff belonging to Group D carry out routine functions and provide support services.

The functions performed by Group B, C, and D officers and staff, are varied and range from general administration to specialized and technical functions. There are variations in the work done in each of these categories depending on the ministry, department, and organization they work for, and this is reflected in the different designations and functions within each group. Though each of these groups has a different channel for recruitment, there is usually a provision for promotion from Group C to Group B and from Group B to Group A. There is also a provision for promotion from Group D to Group C.

However, the Sixth Pay Commission recommended that there should be no further recruitment to Group D and that all the existing pay scales in Group D should be upgraded to Group C. This implied that all the existing incumbents in Group D were upgraded to Group C. At the time the Sixth Pay Commission recommended the abolition of Group D and upgrading of Group D posts to Group C, there were 9.7 lakh sanctioned Group D posts in the Central Government out of which 8.6 lakh were filled up. Fifty-nine per cent of these posts were in the Ministry of Railways and 18.5 per cent were in the civilian section of the Ministry of Defence.

3

The Role of Civil Services

It is widely believed that the current civil service system in India is merely a continuation of the one established during the British rule. However, the tasks they perform are very different. In British India, the civil servants were entrusted with several tasks. These included mapping agricultural lands, making lists of citizen's land rights, fixing land revenues, collecting them, and providing justice by settling disputes. They also initiated various infrastructural activities such as building roads, bridges, and railways, and harnessing the rivers to irrigation.

But the primary task of the civil services in British India was to create and sustain an empire. It was through the civil services that the British cemented their political supremacy in India and were able to impose their will. From Wellesley through the Marquis of Hastings to Dalhousie, the authority of the British in India kept growing and the scope of the operations of empire increased substantially. Clearly, the services of the best and brightest were called for to sustain the empire, maintain its territorial integrity, and impose order.

In retrospect, it seems an almost impossible feat. Some 300 million people were ruled by not more than 1,200 officers of the civil services, assisted by some 50,000 British troops. It was a bluff, but it worked because the administration was light and also because it brought peace and an order India had not known for centuries. That is why the civil services in British India were called the 'steel frame'. They held the empire together.

A lot of care went into choosing these 1,200 officers. The Macaulay Committee Report had made it clear that the interests of the empire demanded that the civil service of colonial India should attract the best and brightest of the British universities. The Report had suggested that the educational background of civil servants in British India should be even better than that of civil servants in England. In the words of the

Committee, 'Indeed, in the case of the civil servant of the Company, a good general education is even more desirable than in the case of the English professional man; for the duties even of a very young servant of the Company are more important than those which ordinarily fall to the lot of a professional man in England.'

The Macaulay Committee also made another important point. The Report pointed out that ideal civil servants should be gifted amateurs who, moving from job to job, can solve any problem on the basis of their knowledge and experience in the government. It is not a coincidence that when the Macaulay Committee Report came out, the 'amateur' was the ideal of what a gentleman should be. For example, there was the cricket match at Lord's between Gentlemen and Players. The Gentlemen were amateurs who came out to play from the centre of the pavilion while the Players, who were professionals, came out of a side door. It was only after World War II that this match was discontinued.

These were the kind of 'gifted amateurs', with a good degree from the best of English universities, who were selected for the civil services and came to India.

But an overwhelming majority of civil servants were Indians. A small group of officers had to maintain control over this large and potentially disruptive group of 'native' employees in the government. For this purpose, the officers used several techniques.

One technique was to have a system by which the small number of officers could be so deployed that they occupied all the important posts at the central, provincial, and district levels of the Empire. Since native subordinates could not be trusted to take decisions, it had to be ensured that they took none of any consequence, or, at the very least, all their decisions had to be approved by the officers. Another technique was to put in place an elaborate set of rules and regulations to control the decision-making powers of the large number of native subordinates.

One more technique was to centralize the decision-making process. Since native subordinates could not be trusted to take decisions, it had to be ensured that they took none of any consequence, or, at the very least, all their decisions had to be approved by the officers. The organizational setup was made hierarchical to ensure a clear-cut chain of command, based on an elaborate system of reporting.

What it meant was that the civil service, and there-fore, the government, had to work within the frame-work of rules and regulations. That is why the role of the civil services is often described as 'regulatory'. However, such a framework was adequate for what the civil services did at the time: The routine work of rev-enue collection, settling disputes, maintenance of law and order, and protecting the interests of the empire.

Though initially the British had set up only the Indian Civil Service (ICS), later they added a Statutory Civil Service and Central Services. In the course of time, the Statutory Civil Service was weeded out and there remained only the ICS and the Central Services. When it was time for the British to leave India, there were nine civil services in the country under the Central Services, besides the ICS.

At the time of independence, there was a debate on what kind of civil service structure the country should have; whether it should be a unified admin-istrative service like the ICS and if so, what should be the modes for its recruitment and control. Most chief ministers were not enthusiastic about a unified administrative service. Some leaders of the Congress Party were opposed to the continuation of the ICS type of civil service because it had been the instrument of British imperial power. Sardar Vallabhbhai Patel, the then Home Minister, supported the case for a unified administrative service. He argued in favour of giving the unified civil service experience at the Central government as well in the states and districts, thus enabling the civil service to be a liaison between the states and the Centre. Patel said:

My own view, as I have told you, is that it is not only advisable but essential if you want to have an efficient service, to have a Central Administrative Service in which we fix a strength as the provinces would require them and we draw a certain number of officers at the Centre, as we are drawing at present. That will give experience to the personnel at the Centre, leading to efficiency in the administration of the district, which will give them an opportunity of contact with the people. They will thus keep themselves in touch with the situation in the country and their practical experience will be most useful to them. Besides, their coming to the Centre will give them a different experience and wider outlook in larger spheres. A combination of these two experiences should make the Service more efficient. They will also serve as a liaison between the provinces and the Government and introduce a certain amount of freshness and vigour in the administration both of the Centre and the Provinces. Therefore my advice is that we should have a Central Service.

Finally, Patel won the round and it was decided that there would be a unified administrative system, by creating two All India Services, the IAS (Indian Administrative Service), and the IPS (Indian Police Service). The Central Services were also continued. The states were to have their own civil services, with a link to the All India Services. The Union Territories were to be served by both the All India and Central Services.

In essence, the basic civil service structure of British India was continued in independent India. The ICS was now called the IAS. The practice of recruiting 'gifted amateurs' to the civil service through a tough, competitive examination was also continued. The location and activities of IAS officers followed broadly the same pattern as those of ICS officers.

In independent India, two broad functions are given to the civil services. The first is formulating policies which pursue objectives specified by the political leadership, and second, its implementation. In the democratic form of government that India adopted, the elected representatives set visions and goals. Policymaking is the process by which civil servants transform these visions and goals into policies, programmes, schemes, and projects. Civil servants who work in the secretariat, whether in the Central or state governments, carry out this function.

Civil servants working at the field level implement these policies. They translate the schemes, programmes, and projects into actions and deliver services to people. They work on behalf of the Central or state governments or the districts, subdivisions, *taluka*s, or blocks. They also work in local bodies such as city corporations, town municipalities, and zilla, intermediate, and *gram* panchayats.

The role of the civil services changed in important ways in independent India. At the time of independence itself, the civil services faced new challenges. The new challenges came as India declared itself to be a welfare state. The welfare of the citizens was viewed as the central task to be performed by the State, and accordingly, the civil service became an instrument for carrying out welfare functions, including the imme-diate challenges of settling refugees and meeting the minimum requirements of their daily lives, safeguard-ing national borders from external aggression, and maintaining internal peace.

The welfare role of the civil service was further rein-forced when the Directive Principles of State Policy were introduced in the Constitution. These principles set out the ideals of a welfare state. They gave general guidelines for legislative and administrative action for promoting the 'welfare of the people'. This was to be done by building and nurturing a social order in which there would be economic, social, and political justice. The Directive Principles also laid down ways in which the welfare of the people could be achieved.

First, it should be ensured that the wealth of society is not concentrated in the hands of a few, but is dis-tributed equitably. Second, there should be adequate means of livelihood for all. There should be no exploi-tation of labour, and labour should not be forced to operate in inhuman conditions. Third, the standard of living should rise for all people. Fourth, all pos-sible steps should be taken to improve public health, with public assistance for the sick. Fifth, free and compulsory education should be provided for all. Sixth, agriculture and animal husbandry should be improved. Seventh, village government should receive encouragement. The goals that the Directive Principles set for the State implied a big change in the role of the civil services.

The Directive Principles also formed the basis for adopting a policy framework for bringing about social change through laws. Accordingly, many progressive laws were passed and the civil services were given the responsibility of implementing these laws. As a result, the role of the civil service in enforcement of rules and maintenance of order (the regulatory role traditionally associated with the civil service) was pushed to the background, and the developmental and transformative role of the civil service became more important.

The Directive Principles also formed the basis for preparing Five-Year Plans to formulate suitable schemes, programmes, and projects for bringing about social change. The civil service was made responsible for implementing these schemes, programmes, and projects. As a consequence, the primary orientation of the civil services became developmental. The First Five-Year Plan document clearly recognized this when it said, 'from the maintenance of law and order and the collection of revenue, the major emphasis now shifts to the development of human and material resources, and the elimination of poverty and want'.

That the role of the civil services changed from purely regulatory to largely developmental is obvious from the priority given to development during the different plan periods. In the First Five-Year Plan (1951–5), the approach adopted was Community Development (CD). CD was the method through which transformation of social and economic life of the villages was to be brought about. Each community project consisted of three development blocks and each block consisted of about 100 villages. The development block was divided into groups of five villages, each of which was looked after by a civil servant working at the village level. The activities in the CD blocks included agriculture, irrigation, roads, health, employment, housing, training, and social welfare.

The CD programme created new roles and responsibilities for the civil services. New ministries and departments in the field of development emerged in the 1950s, each with their own separate hierarchies reaching down to the district and sub-district levels.

The pace and volume of work increased. During this period there was a leap in the numbers of the civil service: from 4.1 million in 1953, it went up to almost 8 million in 1963.

The Second Five-Year Plan (1956–60) focused on industrialization, with the public sector poised to reach commanding heights. It was believed that industrialization was the key to reducing poverty and that a planned economy was essential to industrializing rapidly and achieving self-sufficiency. An industrial licensing system was introduced to give licences for opening up new industries. There was a new system of import substitution, which made imports difficult by permitting selective access to them. A system of tariff was introduced. There was also a new system of quality and price control, which meant discretionary quotas and allocations.

The implementation of these policies for rapid industrialization meant a big role for civil servants. They were put in charge of the industrial licensing system, the system of import substitution, the tariff system, and the system of quotas and allocations. A dominant public sector, considered a symbol of advancement, provided the opportunity for the civil services to

49

manage its undertakings, which were created to achieve rapid industrialization. State control over key industries and regulation of the private sector greatly expanded the role of the civil services.

Starting with the Third Five-Year Plan (1960–5), there were two important changes in the priorities of the government. First, it was the encouragement given to agriculture. In the 1950s, agriculture had been neglected because it was thought that the potential of agricultural exports was limited. Such neglect of agriculture was reversed by encouraging production of new seeds and fertilizers, stepping up agricultural credit, and accelerating rural electrification. The result was the successful Green Revolution that raised the level of food-grain production very appreciably. By the 1970s, India was self-sufficient in grain. The civil service had a big role to play in this development.

The second change was in tightening the control of the State over every aspect of the economy. With the objective of abolishing poverty, private banks were nationalized, trade was further regulated, price controls were imposed on a wide range of products, and foreign investment was controlled. All these meant the government started exercising greater control over the economy and the civil service had a key role to play in these efforts.

Starting with the Third Five-Year Plan, it was also planned that big programmes of rural work would be taken up, for creating employment as well as for utilizing the substantial manpower resources in the rural areas. This would ensure rapid economic development of the country. In fact, the focus of the Third Five-Year Plan was on strengthening the rural economic structures so that a lasting solution to unemployment and underemployment could be provided.

During the Fourth Five-Year Plan (1969–73), policymakers realized that a frontal attack on poverty was necessary in order to eradicate it. For this purpose, the rural areas of the country became the laboratory for several experiments, and the 1970s became a watershed in introducing a series of new programmes to eradicate poverty. A threefold approach was followed, which included (a) creating an income-generating asset base for self-employment of the rural poor, (b) opportunities for wage employment, and (c) area development programmes in backward regions of the country.

The examples of such poverty eradication programmes are: Rural Works Programme, Drought

Prone Areas Programme, and Programmes for Small and Marginal Farmers. The experience gained from the implementation of these programmes was used in successive plan periods either for modifying or reformulating poverty eradication programmes. The civil services were the agents implementing these programmes.

During the years 1951 to 1977, the civil services had a diversified role. They participated in the administration of public sector undertakings, regulated the activities of the private sector, and formulated and implemented social and economic policies for elimination of poverty, development of rural areas, provision of minimum needs and essential commodities, combating inflation, monetary management, reduction of gender gap, and elimination of social inequalities. It was an overwhelming role, but the important thing to note is that the civil services had made the transition from being a purely regulatory agency to both a developmental and regulatory agency.

During the period from 1977 to 1991, the stringent controls on imports and industrial licensing were gradually relaxed, and this stimulated industrial growth. The scope and coverage of poverty eradication programmes were expanded, particularly of the rural employment schemes. The expenditure on these schemes was huge, because it meant a whole lot of subsidy from the government. There were many elections during this period, and each election contributed to a further increase in the scope and content of these developmental schemes. The result was the government treasury was beginning to run dry. In the early 1980s, the government had its first experience of serious resource crunch, which deepened towards the end of the 1980s.

By mid-1991, a new government came to power, and India's foreign exchange reserves were virtually exhausted. Rising interest payments on foreign debt meant that neither the Central nor state governments could afford to pay subsidies on the developmental programmes or take up heavy public investment. It became necessary for the government to get private and foreign investment for the purpose.

This led to the emergence of a new economic policy in 1991, which saw a rollback of the State in economic activities and also, the adoption of policies to create a favourable environment for private sector participation, and contraction of public sector undertakings.

The government abolished most industrial and import licensing, devalued the rupee, reduced import tariffs, liberalized the financial sector and foreign investment, and allowed private investment in areas earlier reserved for the government. This reform process changed the role of the State from principal investor to facilitator of entrepreneurship. In other words, the civil services were required to play a new role: That of the facilitator.

On the whole, the role of the civil services has diversified since the time the country became independent. It is now a mix of regulatory, developmental, and that of a facilitator. The important question is, how have the civil services fared in these multiple roles? In their regulatory role, they have fared well. They have contributed to stability in terms of maintenance of peace, conduct of fair elections, and preservation of the unity of the nation. It must be said to the credit of the civil services that they have been instrumental in providing unity, stability, and order in a country that is prone to ethnic violence, disorder, and fissiparous tendencies.

In its developmental role, the performance of the civil services has been a mixed bag. In terms of economic growth, India's performance now is impressive.

During the last few years, the growth rate has averaged almost 9 per cent, making it one of the fastest growing economies in the world. This suggests that the country is now at a point where it can achieve sustained economic expansion that has the potential to bring significant improvements in the lives of the people. If this growth rate is sustained, it will put India on the path to becoming one of the key players in the world.

But a major weakness in the functioning of the civil services is that the benefits of this growth have not reached many groups in the society, especially the Scheduled Castes, Scheduled Tribes, and minorities. Gender inequality remains a big problem and some of the changes taking place in the country have had an adverse effect on women. The percentage of the population below the poverty line has come down to 26 per cent. However, not only is this still high, but also the rate of decline in poverty has not been commensurate with the rate of growth in the economy.

Indicators of human development such as literacy and education, and maternal and infant mortality rates have shown steady improvement, but they also suggest that progress is slow and India lags behind several other Asian countries. While literacy rates have gone up, the number of illiterate persons is still very high, making India the country with the highest number of illiterate persons in the world. India's maternal and infant mortality rates are much higher than those of the countries in East Asia, showing poor access to essential healthcare services. Almost half of the country's population suffers from severe malnutrition.

In spite of the impressive growth of the economy, agriculture has grown very slowly. This has widened the rural–urban divide, and has also contributed to severe distress in some rural pockets. Total employment has improved in recent years but the labour force has grown even faster, leading to an increase in the unemployment rate. Permanent employment in the organized sector has decreased.

Economic growth across regions in the country has not been balanced, with some of the most backward areas yet to experience any significant growth. The delivery of essential social services at the grassroots level is poor. In fact, a much higher level of human development can be achieved if only the delivery system is improved.

As regards the facilitator's role, there have been significant problems. For example, the provisions of the 73rd and 74th amendments to the Constitution provide for passing on power to the elected members of the local bodies. These amendments have brought about a local governance system in which people participate, regulate, and monitor how agreed-upon things are done. The previous developmental administration in the district was one centred on the Collector, with developmental programmes implemented by civil servants. The new system has reduced the role of the Collector and other civil servants, and brought in new institutions such as the zila, intermediate, and gram panchayats. This has altered the role of the civil servants working at the district and local levels from that of implementers to facilitators. Unfortunately, most civil servants working at the field level are yet to come to terms with their diminished role.

In addition, in the last two decades there have been important changes in the system of public service delivery. Now, many private sector organizations and non-governmental organizations (NGOs) are associated with public service delivery functions, which used to be done by the civil services before. Such association, involving a wide range of players from the non-government sectors, has called for two changes in the functioning of the civil services: (a) The civil services are important, but they cannot operate alone, and (b) the civil services can no longer give orders to these players from the non-governmental sectors. This means that the civil services are in partnership with these players in delivering public services. The civil services are still grappling with their changed role and responsibilities in such a partnership model.

On the whole, the changes that India has experienced in its economic, political, and social structure since independence have affected the role of the civil services in many ways. More importantly, there have been changes in the way both citizens and elected representatives think of the role of the civil service. There has been a shrinking of the direct role of the civil service in delivering public services and it has to work in partnership with the NGOs and the private sector. The challenges have been many and various demands have been placed. All these have transformed the role of the civil services.

4

Recruitment and Training

In its long evolution, the civil services in India have progressed from what essentially was an elitist service in British India to services that now represent the entire social spectrum. This is a positive development. In their representative character, the civil services in India now have a good number of people from rural areas and disadvantaged backgrounds. This has been a net gain for the civil services because candidates from these backgrounds have a keen understanding of the issues, constraints, and problems faced by people in rural areas and disadvantaged sectors.

All civil servants in India are recruited on the basis of merit, through competitive examinations. There is a system of reservation of posts to the extent of 50 per cent in all categories of the civil services in favour of members belonging to the Scheduled Castes, Scheduled Tribes, and Other Backward Classes. This means that candidates from reserved categories compete among themselves within those categories. For example, a candidate from the Scheduled Tribes category competes with other candidates from the same category.

Candidates are recruited for a wide variety of positions in the civil service through various institutional mechanisms. The Union Public Service Commission (UPSC) is the agency that recruits candidates for the All India Services and Central Services. A similar role is played by the State Public Service Commissions for the state governments. In addition, the Staff Selection Commission recruits personnel for other positions in the Central Government. Individual departments in the governments are also authorized to recruit certain categories of personnel.

Union Public Service Commission

The Union Public Service Commission (UPSC) is a constitutional body in the sense that the Indian Constitution provides for the creation of a UPSC to recruit civil servants. The UPSC recruits civil servants for the All India Services and Central Services belonging to Group A and B.

The process of recruitment to the All India and Central Services is called the Civil Services Examination. It consists of three sequential stages: (a) Preliminary examination for selecting candidates for the civil services (main) examination, (b) main examination (written examination followed by an interview) for selecting candidates for entry into the civil services, and (c) post-training test at the end of the Foundation Course in the training academy, including an interview by a board constituted by the UPSC.

The structure of the Civil Services Examination has the following components. The preliminary examination (objective type) consists of a general studies paper carrying 150 marks and an optional subject carrying 300 marks. The main examination has one paper in English carrying 300 marks, one paper in an Indian language carrying 300 marks, two papers in general studies carrying 300 marks each, an essay paper carrying 200 marks, and four papers in two optional subjects carrying 300 marks each. The interview has 300 marks. The minimum educational qualification to compete in the Civil Services Examination is a graduate degree.

The competition is quite tough. For example, in the year 2006, 3.84 lakh candidates applied for civil service positions, out of which the number of candidates who actually appeared was 1.96 lakh. Only 474 candidates were finally selected. This means that only 0.12 per cent of those who appeared for the examination were successful. Going by the success rate, it is clear that the civil services have been able to attract the brightest of the educational system in India. In fact, the competition has become tougher over the years. For example, the success rate for the year 1950 was 8.58 per cent while for the year 1970, it was 6.36 per cent. For the year 1990, the success rate was 0.59 per cent and it had come down to 0.12 per cent in the year 2006.

In addition to the Civil Services Examination, the UPSC conducts competitive examinations for other specialized civil services such as the Indian Forest Service, Indian Economic Service, Indian Statistical Service, and Indian Engineering Services. Only those candidates who have the prescribed graduate qualification (or post-graduate) are eligible to appear for these examinations.

The age range for all these services is twenty-one to thirty years, with a relaxation of three years for candidates from the Other Backward Classes, and five years for candidates from the Scheduled Castes and Scheduled Tribes. The permissible number of chances is four for candidates from the general category, seven for candidates from the Other Backward Castes, and no restriction for candidates from the Scheduled Castes and Scheduled Tribes.

Other Modes of Induction into the All India Services

At present, the recruitment to the All India Services consists of (a) 66.66 per cent by direct recruitment of candidates by the UPSC on the basis of a competitive examination, (b) 28.33 per cent by promotion from the state civil services, and (c) 5 per cent by selection from other services of the state governments.

For example, for the state of Karnataka, the total strength of IAS officers is 259, out of which 181 posts are filled by direct recruitment through the UPSC, and seventy-eight posts are filled by promotion from the state civil services. Of these seventy-eight posts, sixty-seven posts are filled by promotion of officers from the Karnataka Administrative Service and eleven posts are filled by promotion of officers from the other state civil services of Karnataka (who do not belong to the Karnataka Administrative Service).

The general practice is that officers of the state civil service get inducted into the IAS after about eight to twenty-five years of service, there being wide variations across states. For promotion from other services in the state government, officers who are of outstanding merit and ability and hold gazetted posts in a substantive capacity are considered. These officers should not belong to the administrative service and should have completed eight years of service.

Groups B and C

In the Central Government, there is no direct recruitment at the Group B (gazetted) level for either the general administration services or for specialized services. Employees reach the level of Group B only by promotion. For the taxation departments, Group

B officers are the Income Tax Officers, Excise and Customs' Superintendents and Customs' Appraisers; for the postal department, it is the Postmaster; and in the general administration setup, the key Group B officer is the Section Officer.

Staff Selection Commission

The Staff Selection Commission of the Central Government was established in 1977. It has a nation-wide network of nine regional and sub-regional offices. The regional offices are located at Allahabad, Bengaluru, Chennai, Guwahati, Kolkata, Mumbai, and New Delhi. The sub-regional offices are located at Chandigarh and Raipur.

Initially, only the recruitment for posts in Group C (non-technical) was being done by the Staff Selection Commission. Later, the Staff Selection Commission was also entrusted with the task of recruiting for Group B (non-gazetted, both technical and non-technical) posts in various ministries and departments of the Central Government, and their attached and subordinate offices except for those made by the Railway Recruitment Board.

The Staff Selection Commission conducts recruitment to various categories of posts for which candidates are required to possess a graduate degree. The Commission holds a combined graduate level examination for various Group B posts like Income Tax Inspectors, Central Excise Inspectors, Central Bureau of Investigation (CBI) Inspectors, Assistants, Customs' Appraisers, and so on. A preliminary examination in the objective format is held, followed by a written (main) examination consisting of three to five papers. The screened candidates are called for an interview.

In the examination held by the Staff Selection Commission, about 10 lakh candidates appear in a year, out of which the selected candidates are in the range of 10,000 to 30,000. The process of examination takes more than a year from the date of advertising the posts to the final selection. The delay is because of the number of stages in which the examination is conducted.

In addition, the Staff Selection Commission conducts three separate examinations for the posts of Sub-Inspectors in Central Police Organizations, Tax Assistants in the Income Tax Department, and Section Officer (Audit) in the office of the Comptroller and

Auditor General. For all these three examinations, the candidates should have a graduate degree. The Commission also conducts examinations for recruitment of Junior Engineers (Technical Group C posts) in the Central Public Works Department, Junior Hindi Translators, and Statistical Investigators, for which the eligibility is a graduate degree.

Although a large proportion of these jobs for which the Staff Selection Commission does the recruitment require the candidates to possess a graduate degree, the prescribed age limit varies from post to post.

The Staff Selection Commission holds an annual combined matriculation-level examination for recruitment of Lower Division Clerks and stenographers (which are Group C posts). The prescribed qualification for candidates is matriculation or equivalent. On an average, seven lakh candidates appear for this examination. The candidates are first screened through a preliminary examination in the objective format and those who qualify appear for a written test. Candidates who have cleared the written test appear for a skills test, the contents of which vary according to the post. Interviews are not a part of this process.

State Civil Services

On the pattern of the examinations conducted by the UPSC, the Public Service Commissions in the states conduct examinations to select candidates for the state civil services. The Constitution of India provides for the constitution of State Public Service Commissions, and to that extent these Commissions are constitutional bodies. These Commissions conduct competitive examinations to recruit civil servants of the state governments in various categories belonging to Groups A, B, and C.

Age of Entry and the Number of Attempts

The age of entry to the All India Services and Central Services, for which the UPSC does the recruitment, is kept at twenty-one to thirty years, with a relaxation of three years for candidates from the Other Backward Classes and five years for candidates from the Scheduled Castes and Scheduled Tribes. The upper age limit for writing the civil service examination in the 1960s and the early 1970s was twenty-four, with a relaxation of five years for candidates belonging to the Scheduled Castes and Scheduled Tribes. During the last four decades, there has been a progressive increase in the upper age limit.

As a result of the increase in upper age limit, there has been a change in the age profile of the fresh entrants to the All India Services. While the average age of a fresh entrant was about twenty-four years in the 1960s and the early 1970s, it is now more than twenty-seven years. While the difference in the average age at entry is only three years, its impact on the system of values and beliefs that the civil servants bring into the services is significant. It is difficult for civil servants entering at a later stage to adapt to the core values demanded in the civil services.

The number of times a candidate is permitted to appear in the Civil Services Examination has also gone up. Presently, it is four for candidates belonging to the general category, seven for candidates from the Other Backward Classes, and unlimited for candidates from the Scheduled Castes and Scheduled Tribes. The larger number of permissible attempts combined with higher upper age limit means that a large number of candidates continue to appear repeatedly in the Civil

Services Examination over a long period of time. Apart from being a waste of vital human resources, this places a premium on cramming and memorization rather than intelligence and analytical abilities.

Allotment of Cadres to the All India Service Officers

The All India Service [Indian Administrative Service (IAS), Indian Police Service (IPS), and Indian Foreign Service (IFS)] officers are allotted to different states where they spend their entire official career except for the period they are on deputation to the Central government. Till 2007, the allotment of cadres was based on a combination of merit-based system of insiders (candidates who originally belong to the state) in fulfilment of their choice of home state, and a random roster system for those who do not qualify for their home state. In 2008, the government formulated a new Cadre Allocation Policy.

The Cadre Allocation Policy of 2008 seeks to achieve a balance between the need for posting civil servants to different parts of the country and the preference given by civil servants. The highlight of the policy is that civil servants are allocated to different cadres primarily on the basis of merit and their preferences. This, however, is subject to the reservation roster and the underlying principle of maintaining a ratio of 1:2 between insiders and outsiders.

Training Policy

The Government of India put in place a National Training Policy in 1996. The Policy emphasizes that training should be given to all rungs of the civil service starting from the lowest, at the rudimentary level, to the highest, in policymaking. For the purpose of training, the civil services are divided into three levels.

First is the lowest level of the civil services that work at the delivery stage. They are mostly members of the Group D services and the lower stages of Group C services. Second are the supervisory levels and the middle management/administrative levels (they are mostly members of the Group B services, but also consist of higher stages of Group C at one end and the lower stages of Group A at the other end). At the third level are Group A services and All India Services at the administrative/management level.

The National Training Policy also describes how the training activities of the civil servants are to be funded. It stipulates that each department should set apart 1.5 per cent of its salary budget, which is to be used only for training purposes and is not to be diverted for any other purpose.

Training for the Civil Service

All those selected for Group A services are currently required to undergo a two-year induction training. For some services like the Indian Forest Service, the duration of the induction training is longer. The content of the training programme varies from service to service. Induction training for the All India Services and Central Services Group A consists of a Foundation Course and a Professional Course. The Foundation Course is common to the IAS, IPS, and other Central Services Group A. Officers of some technical services like the Indian Economic Service and the Indian Statistical Service also participate in the Foundation Course.

For the non-Group A services, the pattern varies. While some have mandatory induction training, others do not and report directly to their departments for posting. The latter are expected to learn on the job.

Foundation Training

As the name suggests, the Foundation Course provides the foundation for a career in public service. It is a bridge between the academic world of college education and actual governance. The main objectives of the Foundation Course are: (a) Developing a sense of bonding among civil servants belonging to different services, (b) fostering the attitudes and values that every civil servant should possess, and (c) imparting a basic understanding of the environment and functioning of the administration.

Spread over a duration of 15 weeks, this course is conducted at the Lal Bahadur Shastri National Academy of Administration, Mussoorie. A major portion of the training period (12 out of 15 weeks) is devoted to course work and three weeks to village study and extracurricular activities like trekking and river rafting essentially aimed at promoting leadership development and team building. The subjects taught include management, economics, public administration, law, political concepts and the Constitution of India, Indian history and culture, and computer science.

Officers belonging to the All India Services and Central Services Group A, whose recruitment is done by the UPSC through the Civil Services Examination, are required to undergo the Foundation Training. However, those recruited for most of the technical services, for example through the Indian Engineering Services Examination, are not required to undergo the Foundation Training. In many of the services, officers attend the Foundation Course, though it is not mandatory. Foundation training is also imparted by the Institute of Secretariat Training and Management (ISTM) for officers serving in the Central Secretariat.

Professional Training for All India Service and Central Services Group A

The remaining part of the two-year induction training is spent on professional training where civil servants are given inputs that are specific to their jobs. This is to equip them for the kind of assignments they are likely to have during the first ten years of their career. Professional training is given by a training institute set up for each service. Among these training institutes are the National Police Academy at Hyderabad, the Railway Staff College at Vadodara, the National Forest Academy at Dehradun, the National Academy for Direct Taxation at Nagpur, the Audit and Accounts Staff College at Shimla, and so on.

The Lal Bahadur Shastri National Academy of Administration, Mussoorie is the professional training institute for civil servants belonging to the IAS. The professional training course for IAS officers is divided between the Lal Bahadur Shastri National Academy of Administration and the state cadre to which the IAS officer is allotted. The training in the Academy is for a period of 30 weeks during which the broad contents of public administration, law, economics, management, political concepts, and the Constitution of India are taught.

The training in the state cadre for IAS officers is for 52 weeks. It focuses on understanding the laws of the state, administrative practices, socio-economic conditions, history, culture, language, land revenue system, and so on. The officers are usually attached to a district, where the Collector mentors the officer during this phase. There are several attachments to different offices, usually those that the officer would supervise during his/her initial assignments. These attachments help the officer to appreciate the working conditions in such offices and thereby help him/her to be a better supervisor in the years to come.

The professional training for other services focuses on a more subject-specific set of inputs in keeping with the requirements of the future assignments of the civil servants. For example, the professional course for Income Tax officers is conducted over a period of 16 months at the National Institute of Direct Taxes in Nagpur. During the course of the training, professional inputs are given on accountancy, tax laws, business laws, company law, property law, partnership law and Hindu law. After 10 to 11 months of professional training, the officers have eight to ten weeks of on-the-job training. During these sixteen months, the officers also have a three-week industrial attachment and a three-week attachment to an income-tax office.

The training of the Customs and Excise officers is done at the National Academy of Customs and Excise and Narcotics, Faridabad. The training period of 16 months is broadly divided into two modules of eight months each, one related to Excise and the other related to Customs. During the modules, the officers have an attachment at a regional Customs House for two months and also an attachment with preventive formations for one month. In the Excise module, the officers have an attachment of two months with the Excise regional ranges and an industrial attachment of one month. Officers are given intensive inputs in subjects like customs and central excise laws, international trade, accountancy, international conventions and treaties, and public administration.

Mid-career Training

The need for mid-career training is based on the idea that as the civil servant progresses in his/her career, there would be changes in the nature of his/her job. With respect to civil servants belonging to the IAS, it has been the experience that during the first eight to ten years of service, his/her job relates to implementation and coordination of schemes and programmes at the field level. During the next eight to ten years, when the IAS officer moves to higher positions, the nature of his/her job changes to project/programme formulation and management of programmes on a state-wide basis. At still higher levels, the IAS officer is concerned with formulation of policy. Each of these is a set of specialized functions and demands special skills that cannot be learnt on the job.

The current programme of mid-career training for civil servants falls into two categories: compulsory training and optional programmes. Compulsory training is one that the civil servant has to undergo on a compulsory basis. Optional programmes are those that a civil servant opts for, but may or may not be selected for the programme. Mid-career training programme (compulsory training) is a mandatory requirement for further promotion at certain stages in an IAS officer's career. Participation in a mid-career training programme does not qualify the officer for promotion but non-participation debars him/her from promotion.

COMPULSORY MID-CAREER TRAINING

The compulsory mid-career training for IAS officers is in three phases. In the first and second phase, the duration of the mandatory training is eight weeks. In the first phase, the training takes place between the seventh and ninth year of service. In the second phase, the training takes place between the 14th and 16th year of service. In the third phase, the duration of the training is four weeks, and the training takes place between the 26th and 28th year of service.

The compulsory mid-career training of the Indian Revenue Service (Income Tax) is done in two stages. First, when the officers are promoted from one level to the higher level (for example, on promotion to Joint Commissioner, Commissioner, and Chief Commissioner level). These courses are conducted to equip the officers for the requirements of their future assignments. The duration of these courses varies from three to 15 days.

Second, batch-wise training of the officers of the Indian Revenue Service is conducted at the end of 15th year of service and, the other, at the end of 25th year of service. The duration of these batch-wise courses is three days. During the course, the officers are acquainted with the current best practices and methods in the field of tax administration.

OPTIONAL PROGRAMMES

In addition to compulsory programmes, there is a wide choice of optional programmes, which all Group

A officers can attend. The examples of such optional programmes are: (a) Short and long-term training programmes abroad under the scheme of 'Domestic Funding for Foreign Training', (b) higher studies abroad on study leave, (c) one-year Masters programmes on public policy at the Indian Institute of Management, Bangalore and Management Development Institute (MDI), Gurgaon, (d) advanced programme in public policy and administration run by the Indian Institute of Public Administration, New Delhi, and (e) a one-year programme run by the National Defence College, New Delhi. These courses involve a selection process and therefore, not all civil servants who apply for these courses get selected.

Training of Groups B and C

Induction Training

On joining the particular service, some Group B and C employees are given training. The type and intensity of such training vary from service to service. In several departments/organizations, the practice followed is that civil servants undergo rigorous training and it is only after this that they are assigned responsibilities. The Central Police Organizations, Central Board of Direct Taxes, and Central Board of Excise and Customs are good examples of organizations in which officials are given professional training before they are formally inducted into service.

The Central Board of Direct Taxes has regional training institutes where Tax Assistants and Income Tax Inspectors are given technical training. On induction, a Tax Assistant in the Income Tax Department is given training for five weeks, of which two weeks are for specialized income tax computer application training. Newly inducted inspectors are imparted training at a 12-week induction programme, which has components of professional training and some modules of generalized training similar to a Foundation Course.

Similarly, the staff selected for the Customs and Central Excise and Indian Audit and Accounts Service are given training before they are posted to formal positions. Group B and C staff is trained at their regional training institutes and regional training centres, respectively. The training imparted is in the nature of induction courses with emphasis on technical subjects.

In the Central Secretariat Service, assistants are given foundational and professional training after joining the service. This is also the case with the Central Secretariat Stenographers' Service and lower grades in the Central Police Organizations. The Institute of Secretariat Training and Management (ISTM), which gives training to Group B and C officers of the Central Secretariat cadres, has put in place a number of courses and training programmes for various grades.

Mid-career Training

There is no structured mid-career training for any of the Group B and C services. The ISTM has recently introduced mid-career training programmes for various categories of the Central Secretariat Service officers, including the stenographic services. In the few cases where mid-career training programmes are conducted, they are not compulsory and performance during training is not evaluated. As a result, such training is not treated with the degree of seriousness that it deserves.

In general, training efforts are largely focused on the senior civil services, and very little money or effort goes into training the middle and lower levels of government such as Group B and C. In fact, these levels are important because they are the citizens' interface with the government and the image of the government is made or marred by the way a village accountant, a *gramsevak*, a police constable, or an extension officer functions. It is at these levels that civil servants need motivation-building exercises because they are the ones whose prospects of promotions and other forms of reward are limited.

State Governments

At the level of the state governments, there are a number of training institutions providing induction as well as mid-career training to civil servants. At the apex level, the states have established Administrative Training Institutes for training civil servants of the state governments. Some states have established District Training Institutes at the district level for training functionaries at the rudimentary level. For secretariat employees, there is the secretariat training institute.

TRAINING INSTITUTIONS

Training programmes for civil servants are conducted in a large number of government training institutions at the level of the Central and state governments. Today almost all major civil services in the country have a national level training institute or academy. Some organizations like the Indian Railways have established a network of training institutions for training civil servants of different categories.

After economic liberalization in the 1990s, training institutions have tried to re-orient their training programmes in view of the changed priorities. Attention is now paid to good governance, transparency and objectivity in administration, democratic decentralization through the *panchayati* raj institutions, creation of a congenial environment for infrastructural and industrial development, and a citizen-centric approach.

In addition, a large number of academic institutions are now imparting mid-career training programmes. However, a high-quality educational institution may not always turn out to be a high-quality training facility for civil servants. This is because academic institutions are not always in a position to design training programmes with the right mix of theoretical and practical inputs that are relevant for the civil services.

5

Placement of Civil Servants

The Constitution of India provides that rules should be made for the transaction of business of the Government of India. Accordingly, two sets of rules have been made: (a) The Government of India (Allocation of Business) Rules, and (b) the Government of India (Transaction of Business) Rules. The Allocation of Business Rules allocates the business of the government among different departments, which are assigned to the charge of various ministers. The Transaction of Business Rules defines the authority, responsibility, and obligations of each department regarding disposal of business allotted to it.

These Rules, combined with the Manual of Office Procedure, lay down the structure of the Government of India. The structure consists of two levels:

(a) departments, and (b) attached and subordinate offices. The department is responsible for formulating policies for the businesses allocated to it and the execution and review of these policies. Where the execution of policies requires action in the field, organizations called attached and subordinate offices are set up. Attached offices are responsible for implementing the policies of the department to which they are attached. Subordinate offices are the field organizations responsible for the detailed implementation of the policies made by the department. They function under the direction of the attached office, or where the volume of implementation of work is not large, directly under the department.

A department is divided into wings, divisions, branches, and sections. A department is headed by a Secretary, while a wing is headed by a Special Secretary/Additional Secretary/Joint Secretary. The divisions, in turn, are placed under the charge of a Director/Deputy Secretary. In the chain of command, a Director/Deputy Secretary reports to the Joint Secretary, who, in turn reports to the Additional Secretary/Special Secretary/Secretary of the Department. The Director/Deputy Secretary is assisted by an Under Secretary.

The Under Secretary is assisted by a Section Officer, and the Section Officer by assistants.

Placements

The Appointments Committee of the Cabinet decides on senior appointments in the Government of India. Appointments and postings of officers are made under the Central Staffing Scheme, which provides the mechanism for selection and placement of officers to senior administrative posts of the Government of India. While some posts of Deputy Secretary and Under Secretary are filled in accordance with the rules of the Central Secretariat Services, other posts are filled up by officers of the All India Services and Central Services Group A.

The Central Staffing Scheme is designed to fill the need for fresh inputs at senior levels in policy planning, formulation of policy, and implementation of programmes from different sources: the All India Services and Central Services Group A. The services of scientific and technical personnel and professionals in the field of statistics, law, and medicine are similarly obtained from officers serving for specific periods on deputation and who return to their respective cadres at the end of their tenure. This two-way movement is of mutual benefit to the service cadres and the Government of India.

Placements under the Central Staffing Scheme

Postings of officers of the rank of Under Secretary, Deputy Secretary, and Director are done by the Department of Personnel and Training, and a large majority of these officers are from the Central Secretariat Services. Members of the All India Services and Central Services Group A are generally not posted at the level of Under Secretary, positions which are staffed by officers from the Central Secretariat Service. Officers from the All India Services and Central Services Group A are posted at the levels of Deputy Secretary, Director, Joint Secretary, Additional Secretary, Special Secretary, and Secretary.

The Department of Personnel and Training invites nomination of officers for being posted as Deputy Secretary, Director, and Joint Secretary from the state governments and other services. The names of eligible officers forwarded by these organizations constitute the 'offer list'. For each vacancy the names of three officers are shortlisted, based on the past performance of the officer and his/her suitability for the post.

The list is placed before the Civil Services Board, which, in turn, recommends a panel of names to the concerned department/ministry. The department/ministry selects a candidate out of this list. A similar process is adopted for postings at the level of Joint Secretary, but in this case, the proposal is to be approved by the Appointments Committee of the Cabinet. In the case of Additional Secretary and Secretary, recommendations are made to the Appointments Committee of the Cabinet by the Cabinet Secretary.

Empanelment of Officers

All officers of the All India Services or the Central Services Group A who participate in the Central Staffing Scheme are eligible for assignments in the Government of India. The selection of officers is done through an empanelment system to select the suitable ones. In effect, the empanelment system is a means of quality control: Only the names of officers who have good assessment records are put in a panel and it is from this panel that civil servants are selected to work as Joint Secretaries, Additional Secretaries, and Secretaries in the Government of India.

Panels are prepared separately for the posts of Joint Secretary, Additional Secretary, and Secretary. This exercise is carried out on an annual basis by considering the cases of officers with the same year of allotment as one group. For Joint Secretaries, the Civil Services Board finalizes the panel and gets it approved by the Appointments Committee of the Cabinet. In this work, the Civil Services Board is assisted by a Screening Committee of Secretaries. For preparing the panel, the only record that is considered is the Annual Confidential Record (ACR) of the officer, which, as the name indicates, is an annual assessment made of the officer's work by his superior authorities. The cases of officers who are not included in the panel for a particular year are reviewed together after a period of two years. Another such review is conducted after another two years.

For the posts of Additional Secretary and Secretary, a Special Committee of Secretaries is constituted to assess the ACRs and experience profile of the officers. It evaluates such qualities as general reputation, merit,

91

competence, leadership, and aptitude for participation in the policymaking process. This committee recommends a list of officers for approval of the Appointments Committee of the Cabinet. For preparing the panel for Additional Secretary, there is also a panel of experts which evaluates the ACRs and makes an assessment. This assessment is taken into account by the Special Committee of Secretaries. In case women, members of Scheduled Castes/Scheduled Tribes, and persons from the North East are not included in the panel, action is taken to give a representation to these categories. Cases of officers not included in the panel are reviewed twice in the subsequent two years.

Admittedly, the quality of officers who are empanelled for senior positions at the level of the Central government is better than the average quality of the officers working at the level of the state governments. But certain defects of the empanelment system are often pointed out. First, the system is not transparent (although the list of officers empanelled can be accessed under the provisions of the Right to Information Act, the officers themselves are not officially informed). When the panels are prepared, neither is the officer interviewed nor is there a formal test. The officers are not informed whether they are empanelled or not. The officers who are not put on the panel do not get to know the reasons why they were excluded. It follows, therefore, that officers who are not empanelled do not have an opportunity to make an appeal. Second, the process of empanelment implies that while some officers are not good enough to work for the Central government, they are good enough for the state governments or their respective services.

Transfers

Civil servants are liable to be transferred from one post to another in public interest. The Department of Personnel, which is the nodal agency of the Government of India for personnel function, has issued guidelines from time to time on various issues relating to transfer of civil servants. These guidelines provide policy options within the overall constraints of administrative convenience. Similarly, various ministries and departments of the Government of India and state governments have also formulated detailed guidelines about how transfers are to be made, on the general lines of the instructions issued by the Department of

Personnel. All these guidelines make it clear that the right job should go to the right person, his or her tenure at the post should be at least three to five years, and transfers should be based on adequate grounds.

In the case of the Government of India, these guidelines are generally followed. Most civil servants have tenures of three to five years in particular posts. For example, a Joint Secretary has a tenure of five years and an Additional Secretary has a tenure of three years. In lower posts, too, most civil servants enjoy sufficiently long tenures.

When it comes to the state governments, the position is entirely different. Civil servants are transferred very rapidly from one post to another. A study of civil servants working in the Delhi Administration found that, on an average, civil servants lasted less than a year in one department in the Delhi government. According to the study, in less than five years, there were seven postings of Principal Secretaries in the Departments of Finance and Urban Development, and five postings each of the Commissioners of Excise, Transport, and Food and Civil Supplies in the Government of Delhi. The study observed:

On an average, a bureaucrat lasts less than a year in one Department in the Delhi Government. He or she gets transferred out at a dizzying speed to a whole new office even before he can acquaint himself with the ground realities of his Department. The reason: bureaucrats do not fall in line with what the Chief Minister and Ministers expect of them.

The study tried to assess the impact of such quick transfers. A civil servant who was interviewed said, 'Every time we go to a new department, it takes six months to get to know the staff properly. Then it takes another six months to develop a working understanding. Only then can a department look beyond the procedure and take decisions.' He went on to add that, 'We do not even get the names of the staff right.'

It is not that quick transfers happen only in the case of the state of Delhi. They happen all over the country and all the time. In Mohsina Begum's case, the Allahabad High Court observed,

Whenever a new government is formed, there is a tidal wave of transfers of government servants on the basis of caste or community or monetary considerations leading to total demoralization of the bureaucracy and its division on caste and communal basis, besides the spread of corruption and breakdown of all norms of administration.

Unfortunately, frequent transfers of civil servants continues to be one of the most serious governance problems in India. Civil servants are not allowed to stay long enough in a post to acquire adequate knowledge and experience of the job and the problems they need to solve. They are unable to build the confidence and understanding necessary for administrative leadership. Quick transfers prevent civil servants from staying in a post long enough to introduce and sustain reforms. Worse still, frequent transfers and postings lead to lack of accountability and corruption.

Transfer and Postings of IAS Officers

Not only are civil servants at the lower levels of administration transferred very rapidly from one post to another, but also IAS officers, who are senior. Data on IAS transfers for the period 1978 to 2006 shows that the number of IAS officers spending less than a year in their respective postings ranges from 48–60 per cent of the strength of the IAS. Interestingly, the number of IAS officers who spend more than three years in their respective postings has been consistently less than 10 per cent of the total strength of the IAS.

However, the averages given in the last paragraph do not adequately reflect the scenario in the state governments. This is because the data also includes duration of postings of IAS officers in the Government of India, where, on an average, tenures are relatively stable. This shows that the position is quite bad for IAS officers working for the state governments.

Domain Competency

Domain competency means sufficient expertise in the particular area in which the civil servant works. In other words, domain competency should include sufficient knowledge gained from work experience. While it is true that civil servants can be assigned to any post in any department, and are still expected to deliver, we need to recognize the complex challenges posed by modern administration, in the form of specialized requirements. Meeting such challenges would call for domain competency.

The civil services in India suffer from very brief tenures in most assignments. Civil servants are whirled around so rapidly from one post to another that they have no opportunity to acquire domain competency in the area in which they are posted so briefly. Ideally, while posting civil servants to their assignments, the approach should be to carefully match their skills and backgrounds to the requirements of particular positions. Assigning domains to civil servants early in their career and letting them acquire domain competency should be a key step in achieving this objective.

6

Performance Management

As the performance of a department depends on the performance of individual civil servants working in it, it becomes necessary to evaluate the performance of the individual. For the purpose of such evaluation, the government follows the system of the Annual Confidential Report (ACR). In the ACR system, the achievements of the civil servant are recorded and graded at the end of a pre-set period (usually a calendar year).

The important feature of this system is the complete secrecy of the exercise (that is why it is called confidential), both in process and results. The performance of every civil servant is evaluated annually through his/her Confidential Report, which is an important document for assessing his/her suitability for further advancement. The only exception to this secretive process is that adverse remarks are communicated to the officer reported upon.

At the beginning of the year, the Reporting Officer, who is the immediate superior, sets quantitative/physical targets in consultation with the civil servant whose report he/she is required to write. Performance appraisal is a joint exercise between the civil servant reported upon and the Reporting Officer. While fixing targets, priority is assigned item-wise, taking into consideration the nature and area of work. The Confidential Report is initiated by the civil servant to be reported upon, who gives a brief description of his/her duties, specifies the target set for him/her, achievements against each target, shortfalls, constraints faced, and areas where the achievement has exceeded the target.

For civil servants belonging to the All India Services the system is called the Performance Appraisal System and the assessment report is called the Performance Appraisal Report (PAR). The salient features of this Performance Appraisal System are: Setting of goals in consultation with the appraised civil servant, a numerical grading system (scale of 1 to 10), introduction of a pen picture of the appraised officer, and sharing the entire PAR with the appraised officer.

Comparatively, the Performance Appraisal System for the officers belonging to the All India Services is an improvement on the closed system of ACR. It has the added feature of transparency and involvement of the officer at different levels of the assessment process. It also involves setting goals at the start of the assessment period, reviews during the period, and final assessment against achievement of goals. Finally, performance excellence is indicated by a number (grades of 1–10) to be decided by the Reporting Officer.

In any case, the focus still continues to be on ratings and evaluation, and not on performance planning, analysis, and review of improvements, which should help civil servants perform in a superior manner. The system in India is one of performance appraisal, and not of performance management. Performance appraisal is only one component of the performance management cycle and is the process of assessing the civil servant's performance in the current position. Performance appraisal is a once-a-year affair while performance management is a year-round activity. In addition, performance appraisal focuses on ratings while performance management focuses on the work, assessment by the stakeholders, service levels, productivity, motivation effort, and all such performance-related variables.

Incentives

Civil servants in India are paid according to salary scales that include time-bound increments to the base salary. There is hardly any performance-based incentive available to them. Their salaries are a combination of basic pay and increments plus certain allowances that are admissible depending on the nature of the jobs and duties. In fact, a natural increase in salary is very much guaranteed to civil servants, irrespective of performance.

This has led to a situation where civil servants do not have to exert themselves for improved performance or achievement. There is no motivation for taking risks and delivering a higher standard of performance because, though risk-taking is punished if things go wrong, it is not financially rewarded if things improve. This has led to the development of a culture in which civil servants concentrate on routine observance of procedures without concern for results and performance.

A scheme has been put in place in 2008, which introduces a performance-based incentive over and above the regular salary. The scheme is called Performance-Related Incentive Scheme (PRIS). Under the scheme, an incentive is payable to the civil servant on the basis of his/her performance during the period under consideration. It is based on the principle of reward as per performance.

PRIS is a combination of individual, team, and organization-based incentives. The scheme provides for negative incentives in cases of underperformance. This takes the form of civil servants within the group blocked from getting PRIS if certain parameters are not achieved. PRIS provides for separate, organization-specific weights to be assigned to stakeholder accountability for service gaps. It is a good incentive scheme and is expected to improve performance.

Managing Poor Performance

The other side of performance management is how to manage poor performance. Initiating disciplinary proceedings is the most common mechanism to punish a civil servant for poor performance. However, things are made difficult by the Constitution of India, which requires that a reasonable opportunity should be given to the civil servant to deny the charges made against him/her. It is only after the civil servant has been given that opportunity, and if the enquiry finds him/her guilty, a penalty can be imposed on him/her.

But the matter does not end there. There are legal provisions for appeal, revision, and review. It is only after the civil servant exhausts all these legal remedies available to him that he is allowed to suffer the penalty. The civil servant also has the right to challenge the legality of the order before the Administrative Tribunal, get an interim stay, and then, appeal against the main order. After he exhausts this remedy, the civil servant has the option of exercising his fundamental right as a citizen and approaching the High Court or the Supreme Court for relief.

This is only the process. There are also procedures prescribed about how the departmental enquiry should be conducted. There are twelve stages in a departmental enquiry. These stages start with the preparation of the charge sheet and end with the imposition of a penalty. It has been calculated that the time taken in completing an enquiry is a minimum of three years. To that, if one adds the time taken by the Administrative Tribunal, the High Court, and the Supreme Court, it takes at least 10 years to punish a civil servant for poor performance.

The civil servant in India has remained immune from penalties due to such complicated procedures. These have grown out of the protection given to civil servants in the Constitution against arbitrary action. The enquiry proceedings against a civil servant have to be conducted in accordance with Article 311 of the Constitution, which provides that no civil servant can be punished 'except after an enquiry in which he has been informed of the charges against him and given a reasonable opportunity of being heard in respect of those charges'. Because of this safeguard in Article 311, most departmental enquiries take a long time to complete. As if to compound the matter, most departmental enquiries end in favour of the civil servant due to some lapse in the procedure.

This constitutional safeguard has shielded the non-performing civil servant from punishment, and the result is that such a civil servant cannot be held accountable for his work. The protection given to the civil servant under Article 311 is excessive. No other constitution in the world contains the kind of protection and guarantee that Article 311 provides. When Sardar Vallabhbhai Patel, the then Home Minister, argued before the Constituent Assembly for providing protection to civil servants, his intention was to enable the civil servants to render impartial and honest advice to the political executive without fear. But the way it has worked, Article 311 has created an environment of excessive security without any fear of being punished for poor performance.

That is why, in India, we do not have a tradition of punishing civil servants for poor performance. India is one of the few emerging nations in the world that does not distinguish between performers and non-performers, and allows both the categories to progress in their career without subjecting growth to performance. It is necessary that an enabling environment is created in which improved performance is rewarded and poor performance is punished. It is particularly important for the sake of the government department in meeting its performance target. It is, therefore, imperative to put in place simpler procedures for managing poor performance.

7

Accountability

Accountability can be defined as the obligation of those exercising power to take responsibility for their actions. There are three elements that come together in the notion of accountability: Answerability, enforcement, and responsiveness. Answerability is the need for providing justification for one's actions. Enforcement consists of sanctions that could be imposed if the justification for the action is found to be unsatisfactory. Responsiveness means the ability of those who are held accountable to respond to the demands made on them. On the whole, accountability requires transparency so that actions can be scrutinized and performance assessed.

There can be six types of accountability: Managerial, political, institutional, judicial, social, and professional.

The following diagram illustrates what these different types of accountability mean.

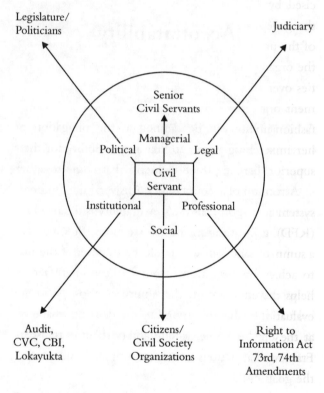

FIGURE 1 Accountabilities
Source: Author.

Managerial Accountability

This is in the form of internal accountability exercised by authorities such as ministers, secretaries to the government, heads of the department, and heads of the units. This kind of accountability is internal to the organization and is exercised by superior authorities over civil servants reporting to them. All government organizations in India operate in a hierarchical fashion in which a civil servant is accountable to his/her immediate superior, and through the immediate superior, to the head of the organization.

A recent addition to the managerial accountability system in India is the Result Framework Document (RFD). Each department now prepares a RFD, giving a summary of the most important results that it intends to achieve during a financial year. Such a document helps the government arrive at an objective and fair evaluation of the organization's overall performance at the end of the year. After six months, the Result Framework and actual achievements are reviewed and the goals in the RFD are reset. Changed priorities are taken into account and unforeseen circumstances are factored in. At the end of the year, an evaluation is carried out against the agreed-upon results specified in the RFD. Civil servants are required to submit the evaluation report to their ministries on the 1st of May and then make it public on their websites to let the public judge their performance.

RFDs not only contain the objectives, policies, programmes, and projects agreed upon, but also success indicators and targets to measure progress. RFDs reflect three basic questions: (a) What are the main objectives of the organization for the year, (b) what actions are proposed to achieve these objectives, and (c) how would someone know at the end of the year the degree of progress made in implementing these actions. The RFD is divided into five sections that include the organization's long-term vision, objectives and functions, *inter se* priorities among key objectives, success indicators and targets, detailed definition of success indicators and methodology of their measurement, and specific performance required from other organizations that is critical for delivering the results.

An important part of the RFD is the organization's long-term vision. As envisaged under the RFD scheme, the vision is a long-term statement that does not change from year to year. However, the RFD

110

scheme emphasizes the need for the employees of the organization to adopt the vision with sincerity. The scheme requires that the leadership in the organization consult a wide cross-section and come up with a vision that should be owned by the employees of the organization. The scheme also requires that the vision should have a time span of five to ten years. If it is less, it becomes tactical, and if it is for twenty-plus years, it becomes difficult for the strategy to relate to the vision.

An RFD is required to specify one or more success indicators or key performance indicators. It covers both qualitative and quantitative aspects of the organization in order to enable evaluation of progress of policies, programmes, schemes, and projects. Sometimes, more than one success indicator may be required to tell the entire story. According to the RFD scheme, success indicators are important management tools for driving improvements in an organization's performance. They should represent the main business of the organization and should aid accountability. If there are multiple actions associated with an objective, the weight assigned to a particular objective should be spread across the relevant success indicators.

Political Accountability

The Indian Constitution provides for the separation of powers between the legislature, executive, and judiciary. Each of these pillars of the State has well-defined areas of operation and jurisdiction. There is an interface between the legislature and the executive at the level of the Council of Ministers, which is collectively responsible to the legislature. But the important point to note is that in India, the legislature cannot perform executive functions and the executive cannot tell the legislature how it should perform its duties.

The Indian Constitution separates the executive into two parts. Under Articles 53 and 154 of the Indian Constitution the executive power of the Union and the states vests in the president and the governor, respectively. The power is to be exercised by the president or governor through officers subordinate to him/her. These officers constitute the permanent civil service or the permanent arm of the executive. The provisions relating to the permanent civil service are laid down in Part XIV of the Constitution. The other part of the executive is the political. The president or governor is required to act according to the aid and advice of the

Council of Ministers. This advice by the Council of Ministers is binding. That being the case, for the civil servants, such advice becomes an order, which they must obey.

The Constitution also provides for the President or Governor to frame rules for the conduct of business of the government. Work is allotted among ministers in accordance with the Business Allocation Rules that the president or governor makes. The manner in which civil servants are required to help the president or governor exercise his/her executive functions is governed by the Rules of Business of the Executive Government.

This means that though the civil servants are subordinate to the President or Governor, they carry out orders of the Council of Ministers in accordance with the rules framed. The Rules of Business of the Executive Government provide for a Secretary to the Government (civil servant) to advise the minister about the course of action proposed in a particular matter and to submit a note which tells the minister about the propriety or legality of his orders. This note may suggest that either such orders not be given or that they may be suitably modified.

The relationship between the civil servant and the minister is organic. The minister has the mandate of the people to govern, but the civil servant has an equivalent constitutional mandate to advise the minister. Once his/her advice has been suitably considered (unless the minister passes an illegal order), the civil servant is bound to implement that order. The minister, on his part, is required to support the civil servant who is implementing his order. So, in the scheme of things, once a law is made or rules and regulations under that law are approved, they apply to everyone, whether he/she is a member of the political executive or of the permanent civil service. A civil servant is required to implement the orders of the government without bias, with honesty, and without fear or favour.

Ultimately, the executive is accountable to the legislature. The legislature holds the executive accountable through several mechanisms, such as questions, debates, adjournment motions, no-confidence motions, calling attention notices, half-an-hour discussions and through the working of the legislative committees like the Parliamentary Standing Committee, the Public Accounts Committee, the Estimates Committee, the Public Undertakings Committee, and so on.

We need to note that political accountability as exercised by the legislatures in India has not been particularly effective. This is because of the fact that that there has been a steady deterioration in both the quality and quantity of deliberations in Parliament and state legislatures. Sittings of Parliament have been low in recent years. For example, in 2008, they were as low as 46 days. This is as compared to the average of 130 days during the 1950s. As a result, there has been a fall in the number of bills passed, questions asked, and debates undertaken.

Other indicators of parliamentary performance are also equally unsatisfactory. For example, the Public Accounts Committee scrutinizes a very small number of audit reports, and civil servants rarely follow up on the recommendations of the Public Accounts Committee. According to the reports of the Comptroller and Auditor General (CAG), out of the 9,000 audit paragraphs tabled in Parliament between 1994 and 2008, over 3,000 are yet to be responded to.

Institutional Accountability

This kind of accountability is exercised by specialist institutions such as the Comptroller and Auditor

General, Central Vigilance Commission, Central Bureau of Investigation, and Lokayukta and other anti-corruption bodies of the state governments. These institutions monitor the activities of civil servants and conduct investigations into their wrongdoings, with the objectives of checking abuse of power and ensuring that their actions are held to account.

Audit

The Indian system of audit provides for post-audit of government accounts. The system of audit is headed by the CAG of India. The CAG is an independent authority created by the Constitution of India. The independence of audit is assured by providing it protection and privileges under the Constitution.

The functions of audit in India are very comprehensive. They consist of audit of all government expenditure incurred from the revenues of the Government of India and state governments. There is also audit of stores and stocks, audit of all receipts, and audit of appropriations to ensure that government grants are spent for the purpose for which they were provided.

In addition, there is administrative audit to ensure that expenditure is supported by orders from the appropriate authority.

Other forms of audit include audit of propriety to find out whether the expenditure has been sanctioned properly after following all the rules and procedures. There is the audit of efficiency to ascertain whether the expenditure has achieved the expected results. There is also audit of accountancy to detect fraud, technical errors, and errors of principle in expenditure. The audit by the CAG covers public sector undertakings and autonomous organizations of the Government of India and state governments.

The Constitution of India requires the CAG to present audit reports to the president of India and governors of the states, who lay them before Parliament and state legislatures. Audit reports are also discussed by the Public Accounts Committees of the legislatures, and the discussion includes examination of witnesses from the executive. A final report is prepared, and presented to the legislatures.

Audit in India has created an impact and acted as an effective instrument of accountability. But it is only post-audit, and in most cases, the time lag between the actual wrongdoing and reporting about it in audit is so big that the wrongdoing is rarely reported in time. The Fifth Pay Commission had this to say,

> Audit should try to be as concurrent as possible. Scandals and scams are known even while they are being planned and executed. If audit draws attention to them forthwith in a well-publicized manner, such scandals can be halted in mid-stride. Post-mortems are useful but can only be conducted when the patient is dead. It is better to cure the patient and try to keep him alive.

Central Vigilance Commission

At the level of Government of India, the Central Vigilance Commission is responsible for dealing with corruption of civil servants. Apart from conducting enquiries and deciding on what punishment should be given to civil servants found guilty of corrupt practices, the Commission advises the Government of India in respect of all matters pertaining to maintenance of integrity in administration.

The Commission is a multi-member body with the Chief Vigilance Commissioner and four vigilance commissioners. The Commission is a statutory body. It has total control over the Central Bureau of Investigation (CBI), which conducts investigations into charges of corruption against civil servants. The Commission also has powers to order enquiries on its own, into charges of corruption against civil servants.

The Commission was originally a one-member body headed by the Central Vigilance Commissioner, and had no statutory status. Statutory status means that an organization is given its status by a law. The Supreme Court directed in 1997 that the Central Vigilance Commission should be given statutory status, and that the Central Vigilance Commissioner should be select-ed by a committee comprising the prime minister, the home minister, and the leader of the opposition in the Lok Sabha, from a panel of outstanding civil servants, and others. In 1998, statutory status was conferred on the Commission so as to ensure a degree of indepen-dence in the functioning of the Commission. Now the Chief Vigilance Commissioner is selected in the manner indicated by the Supreme Court.

The jurisdiction of the Central Vigilance Commission extends to all civil servants working in the Government of India as well as employees of organizations under the administrative control of the Government, including public sector undertakings and nationalized banks. However, for the sake of practical considerations, the Commission advises only on those vigilance cases which involve civil servants of the following categories: (a) Gazetted civil servants (b) board-level appointees in public sector undertakings, (c) officers of the rank of Scale III and above in nationalized banks, (d) officers of the rank of assistant manager and above in the insurance sector, and (e) officers in autonomous organizations or local bodies or societies who are comparable in status to gazetted civil servants in the Government of India.

This does not mean that civil servants of other categories are exempted from the purview of the Commission. The Commission is fully within its powers to call for any individual case in respect of any civil servant, and tender advice as to the appropriate course of action to be taken in such cases.

Complaints against civil servants are received in the Commission either directly or through departments. On confirming that there is a case in the complaints, the Commission gets them investigated either through the CBI or the Chief Vigilance Officer of the department. Handling of the complaints directly received in the Commission is a very small part of its work.

After a complaint is taken up for investigation, it becomes a vigilance case. The departments are required to refer cases to the Commission to obtain its advice usually at two stages. After the investigation is completed by the department or the CBI, the Commission is consulted on the further course of action to be taken (filing a case in a court or dropping the case). This is called first-stage advice.

In cases in which the department recommends that a major penalty be imposed after the first-stage advice, the Commission is consulted again for second-stage advice on completion of the enquiry. The Commission is consulted for second-stage advice in cases in which the department wants to close the case against the civil servant. The Commission is also consulted at other stages of a vigilance case such as consideration by appellate, revising and reviewing authorities.

Central Bureau of Investigation

The CBI is the premier investigating agency of the Government of India in anti-corruption cases. The CBI is headed by a director who is supported by three additional/special directors and 15 joint directors besides a legal advisor and supporting staff. It has offices all over the country. It has three main divisions: (a) anti-corruption division, (b) special crime division, and (c) economic offences division.

The CBI has 800 investigating officers and 200 prosecutors. About 75 per cent of the staff of the CBI is drawn on deputation from police departments, and after they prove their mettle in CBI work, they are given a permanent posting at the CBI. Those who do not make the grade are sent back. Since a large percentage of staff is from the police department who are inducted into the institution after careful scrutiny of their performance, they have good investigative abilities. That is why there is always a demand for the CBI to investigate sensitive cases.

The CBI deals with various types of offences: Corruption, murder, kidnapping, abduction, and economic offences. Interestingly, it was even given the task of examining documents relating to the date of birth of the Chief Justice of the Supreme Court. But anti-corruption work is its core function.

Lokayukta

The first Administrative Reforms Commission had recommended that the institution of Lokayukta be set up at the state level. Accordingly, many state governments passed laws to set up the institution of Lokayukta to investigate allegations and grievances against civil servants, ruling politicians, legislators, staff of local bodies, public sector undertakings, and other organizations of the state government, including cooperative societies and universities. The Lokayukta law generally provides for a member of the public to file specific allegations with the Lokayukta against any civil servant for enquiry. It is also open for the Lokayukta to start an enquiry on its own, into the conduct of civil servants.

The Lokayukta is generally a retired judge of the Supreme Court or the High Court. He/she is appointed for a term of five years. The Lokayukta laws generally provide for a committee consisting of the Chief Minister, Chief Justice of the High Court, Speaker of the House, and Leader of the Opposition in the state legislature to select the Lokayukta. Although the institution of the Lokayukta was set up as a result of the recommendation of the Administrative Reforms Commission, there is a great deal of variation in the structure of the institution across states.

Presently, over seventeen states have Lokayuktas but there is no uniformity in their functions. The Lokayuktas in Maharashtra and Orissa are more of grievance redressal organizations than anti-corruption bodies. In a few states, a wide range of functionaries including the chief minister, vice-chancellors of the universities, and office-bearers of cooperative societies are brought under the purview of the Lokayukta. In most other states, these functionaries are not within the purview of the Lokayukta.

But one common feature is that the investigating staff of the Lokayukta generally consist of police officers who are on deputation from the local police department of the state government. In addition, the Lokayukta has to get the prior approval of the state government for placing any civil servant under suspension or filing a case against him/her in a court.

On the whole, there is an impression that the institution of the Lokayukta has not been given the degree of independence which is necessary for it to function effectively as an autonomous anti-corruption body. The common point in the complaints of the Lokayuktas of various states is that they do not get sufficient information from the government departments, which would enable them to function effectively.

Anti-corruption Bodies of State Governments

Some state governments have vigilance bodies, although the nature and staffing of these bodies vary. While some states have vigilance commissions, others have anti-corruption bureaus as a part of the police department.

The state vigilance commissions, wherever they exist, are patterned on the Central Vigilance Commission. They are headed by a person with the status of a judge of the High Court. The state vigilance commissions are empowered to examine complaints against corrupt civil servants. In conducting investigations, state vigilance commissions are assisted by police officers on deputation from the state governments.

Some states have anti-corruption departments which are extensions of the police department, with some degree of autonomy to function as vigilance organizations. In Rajasthan, for example, the anti-corruption body is called the Rajasthan State Bureau of Investigation. It is headed by a Director General of Police who is on deputation from the police department of the state. He is assisted by an Inspector General of Police, two deputy inspector generals of police, four superintendents of police, six additional superintendents of police, and three deputy superintendents of police, who are on deputation from the police department of the state. The Bureau reports directly to the Chief Minister of the state.

In general, the state vigilance commissions and anti-corruption departments operating at the state level have not been able to demand accountability from civil servants. This is because the investigating staff is drawn from the ranks of the state government itself. In addition, their anti-corruption efforts depend on the will and pleasure of the state government. For example, even in instances where there is a sound case against a civil servant, they have to seek the prior approval of the state government for placing the him/her under suspension or filing a case against him/her in a court.

Lokpal

The first Administrative Reforms Commission had also recommended the establishment of the institution of Lokpal in the Government of India. The Lokpal is supposed to be a watchdog over the integrity of all civil servants and functionaries of the Government of India including the prime minister, other ministers, and members of Parliament.

Right now, there is public agitation for the immediate creation of a Lokpal with powers over all the functionaries of the Government of India including the prime minister, all ministers, members of Parliament, and all civil servants including those belonging to Groups A, B, and C.

Judicial Accountability

The judiciary in India is an important instrument of accountability. By creatively interpreting various provisions of the Indian Constitution, the judiciary in India has become an institution of effective governance. In recent times, it has not only held the executive bodies accountable, but also taken over the supervision of the actual functioning of the executive. The judiciary in India has been at the forefront of holding the government to account. This has been made possible by the proactive stance of the Supreme Court and of a few high courts while hearing public interest litigations (PILs) filed before these courts by concerned citizens, in which the subject matter has often been corrupt practices of civil servants.

The Supreme Court has creatively interpreted Article 124 of the Constitution which provides that the Supreme Court can take steps to enforce decrees and orders that it considers necessary for doing complete justice in any matter pending before it. By doing this, the Supreme Court has succeeded in giving a positive direction to corruption cases involving high functionaries of the government. Judges of the Supreme Court have gone to the extent of personally supervising the process of investigation in these cases if only to ensure that the investigation is not endlessly delayed by the investigating agencies at the behest of influential persons.

The proactive stance of the Supreme Court has created the desired impact in the matter of big scams in which civil servants are involved. But this point needs some clarification in the context of the varieties of official corruption which exist in India. Official corruption can, very broadly, be divided into two general categories. One is the corruption of scams, as in the case of large contracts, and big favours at the higher levels of the government. It is over big scams that the Supreme Court has been successful in demanding accountability from civil servants.

The other variety is retail corruption. This kind of corruption, often done through extortion, is the one that touches the lives of most citizens in the country. Retail corruption is more widespread: Studies conducted by the Public Affairs Centre, Bangalore provide evidence on the extent of retail corruption in India. According to these studies, every fourth person in Chennai ends up paying a bribe in dealing with government agencies such as the urban development authority, electricity board, municipal corporation, and telephone department, while in Bangalore, it is one in eight persons, and in Pune, one in 17 persons. Clearly, retail corruption is widespread and deserves to be addressed with the same degree of seriousness as scams, if not more, because it touches the lives of ordinary citizens in many ways.

For the judiciary to act as an effective instrument of accountability, it has to be efficient in disposing of cases. In this important aspect, the performance of the judiciary has not been encouraging. In 2010, for example, there were 54,600 cases stuck in the Supreme Court, 4.18 million cases in the high courts, and 27.89 million cases in lower (district and subordinate) courts. Out of this, 74 per cent of the cases are less than five years old, and around 26 per cent are more than five years old. At around 8.5 million (26 per cent) the number is still quite formidable.

Social Accountability

In recent years, the civil society in India has become the forum for citizens to make demands for accountability from the civil service. Such accountability has been demanded in a number of ways. Civil society organizations (NGOs and social movements) have been at the forefront of this accountability agenda. The efforts of these organizations are based on getting information about the working of government departments and using the information to get better results in the implementation of government schemes and programmes.

Some of these civil society organizations work in the area of budget analysis and advocacy. The focus of their work is to find out what benefits are going to the poorer sections of the society. For example, Disha (a Gujarat-based NGO), works in the area of analysing the Gujarat state budget to ascertain how the poor, particularly the Scheduled Castes/Scheduled Tribes and people belonging to India's indigenous community, benefit from the money provided in the budget. Similarly, the National Campaign on Dalit Human Rights (NCDHR), which works for promoting Dalit rights, looks at whether the Scheduled Castes benefit from the money kept aside for them in the budget.

Some of the civil society organizations look at the actual results of the implementation of government schemes and programmes. The idea is to hold civil servants accountable for the proper implementation of these schemes and programmes. The methods used are: expenditure tracking surveys, satisfaction surveys, scorecards, and monitoring outcomes.

131

For example, Pratham—an NGO working on elementary education in India—started a programme called Annual Survey of Education Report (ASER) to track learning levels among primary school children. The survey is an exercise to collect data from every district of the country. By using this data, ASER tested the learning levels of school children on the basis of three indicators: reading, comprehension, and arithmetic. By conducting this survey every year, Pratham tracks yearly progress of learning levels across states and is in a position to hold civil servants accountable for the large amount of government money spent on primary education.

Some civil society organizations build capacity in citizens to hold civil servants accountable for their performance. The methods used are social audit and public hearings. Social audit is the process in which villagers get hold of records and expenditure details of a government scheme or programme and compare them with the versions of beneficiaries. This leads to a public hearing where the discrepancies are read out to the assembled villagers, corrupt officials are denounced and sometimes, the money stolen from the scheme or programme is recovered.

Pioneering work in social audit and public hearing has been done by the Mazdoor Kissan Shakti Sangathan (MKSS) in respect of government relief works in several districts of Rajasthan. By using the method of public hearing, Parivartan, an NGO working in Delhi, has been successful in exposing corruption in the Public Distribution System. Now, social audit has officially been made a part of the implementation of the National Rural Employment Guarantee Act (NREGA), which requires that for all the works done under the scheme, audit should be carried out regularly.

Social accountability now plays a crucial role in demanding accountability from civil servants. It also expands the scope of accountability. Those who demand accountability now range from individual citizens to civil society organizations and social movements. The agencies from which accountability is demanded consist not only of civil servants, but elected representatives, regulatory agencies, and even the judiciary.

Another feature of social accountability is that it promotes transparency. For social accountability to work, information about the workings of the government is needed. Access to information becomes the key. More information means more empowerment, and with greater participation, it means a stronger public voice, which, in turn, translates into accountability.

By and large, the civil society and concerned citizens have approached the judiciary for relief. The courts, particularly the Supreme Court and high courts, have acted upon the pleas made by civil society organizations. In addition, some civil society organizations are now members of important government commissions and councils, and acting in that capacity, these organizations have succeeded in making accountability an integral part of government policies and their implementation.

Professional Accountability

The government has also taken some important measures to promote accountability by increasing direct citizen participation in the process of governance. The most important of these initiatives are the 73rd and 74th amendments to the Constitution. These amendments provide for holding regular elections at the town and village level, and for giving substantial administrative powers to local bodies in both urban and rural areas.

The 73rd and 74th amendments have changed the civil servant-dominated local government system into a locally-managed governance system in which people participate, regulate, and monitor. The idea of these amendments was to bring about a system in which local government is made more responsive, and therefore, more accountable. The result has been the creation of hundreds and thousands of people's organizations where none existed before, and these institutions now demand accountability from civil servants working in the local government.

One of the basic ideas of these amendments was to enhance participation of people in the everyday workings of the government at the village level, through the mechanism of *Gram Sabha*. Gram Sabha is the village assembly consisting of all the adult members of the village. Substantial powers have been given to the Gram Sabha to plan and decide what development works should be taken up in the village, and to monitor the implementation of these works. In various other laws that were passed subsequently (for example, the National Rural Employment Guarantee Act and the Forest Rights Act), a lot of importance has been attached to the Gram Sabha. This means that people working through the institution of the Gram Sabha are able to demand accountability from civil servants at the village level.

The government has also put in place several other village-level institutions to enforce accountability. Examples include the Village Education Committee, Village Water and Sanitation Committee, Village Health Committee, and in urban areas, the Resident Welfare Association. All these institutions have been created to make the delivery of government services more responsive to local needs, and to empower the village community to participate in the management of these services and ensure accountability.

The most important action of the government in ensuring accountability was the passing of the Right to Information Act. The Right to Information Act gives every citizen the right to demand and acquire information about public policies and their implementation. Right to information opens up government's records to public scrutiny, thereby helping the citizen to know what the government does and how effectively. It, thus, makes civil servants more accountable.

In fact, the implementation of the Right to Information Act has created new ways in which citizens can demand accountability from civil servants. The governments have now opened up many of their operations to public scrutiny by way of giving information through the Right to Information Act. Two of the biggest government programmes—the National Rural Employment Guarantee Scheme (NREGS) and the National Rural Health Mission (NRHM)— have provisions for disclosing information about their implementation, thus ensuring accountability. The Right to Information Act represents an important opportunity for the citizens of this country to demand accountability from the civil service.

The government has already introduced a bill in Parliament in 2011, called the Citizens Right to Grievance Redress Bill, 2011. This Bill lays down an obligation on the part of every public authority to publish a citizens' charter, stipulating the time within which specified goods shall be supplied and services shall be rendered. The important thing about the Bill is that it gives a right to service to all citizens of India. It stipulates that every individual citizen shall have the right to time-bound delivery of goods and provision of services, and redressal of his/her grievance if the goods and services are not provided.

The Bill casts a legal obligation over civil servants to provide goods and services to citizens through the publication of a citizens' charter. According to the provisions of the Bill, a citizens' charter is a document that declares the obligations, duties, and commitments of a public authority for providing goods and services effectively and efficiently with acceptable standards, time limits, and mechanisms of grievance redressal.

The Bill also provides for a grievance redressal mechanism for non-compliance of the citizens' charter. In terms of the Bill, a complaint can be filed by a citizen for any failure in the delivery of goods or rendering of service that is included in the citizens' charter. The complaint can be filed before an officer of the department who has been designated as the Grievance Redress Officer. In case the grievance is not redressed by the officer, an appeal can be filed before the Head of the Department. The Bill provides for an appeal from the order of the Head of the Department to the State Public Grievance Redressal Commission. An appeal from the order of the State Public Grievance Redressal Commission lies to the Central Public Grievance Redressal Commission.

The Bill provides for penalties to be imposed. The Head of the Department, State Public Grievance Redressal Commission, and Central Public Grievance Redressal Commission have been given the power of imposing a lump-sum penalty on officials responsible for delivery of service or on Grievance Redress Officers for their *mala fide* action. In case these officers are proved to be guilty of *mala fide* action, the Bill provides for disciplinary proceedings to be initiated against them.

The government has also introduced a bill in Parliament in 2011, called the Electronic Delivery of Services Bill, 2011. This Bill provides for electronic delivery of public services by the government to all persons to ensure transparency, efficiency, accountability, accessibility, and reliability in the delivery of such services. In terms of the Bill, electronic service delivery means the delivery of public services or other services through the electronic mode. It includes the receipt of forms and applications, issue or grant of any licence, permit, certificate, sanction or approval, and the receipt or payment of money.

On the whole, several mechanisms exist or are being planned in India for enforcing the accountability of the civil service. The effectiveness of some of these accountability mechanisms, such as, managerial, political, and institutional, has been limited. But what has succeeded is the citizens' role in enforcing accountability, both in terms of who demands it and the mechanisms through which these demands are made.

8

Relationship between the Political Executive and Civil Servants

In a democracy, power vests in the people. This power is exercised through elected representatives who are given the authority by the people to govern them for a specific period. The civil services, due to their knowledge, experience, and understanding of how the government works, assist the elected representatives in making policies and are responsible for implementing them. A parliamentary democracy, like the one we have, usually has permanent civil services, which assist the political executive.

A healthy working relationship between the ministers and civil servants is the key to good governance.

In theory, the minister is answerable to the people through the legislature and the civil servant to the minister. However, impartial civil services are not only responsible to the government of the day, but also to the Constitution to which the civil servants have taken an oath of loyalty. This is the basis on which the respective roles and responsibilities of ministers and civil servants are defined and boundary lines are drawn. But in actual practice, the lines often get blurred, as both sides keep encroaching upon each other's domain.

In the initial years after independence, the relationship between ministers and civil servants was one of mutual respect and understanding. However, in subsequent years, things have changed. While the advice rendered by some civil servants to their ministers was neither objective nor impartial, some ministers began to resent the advice that did not fit in with their short-term political interests. There was, thus, a tendency on the part of the ministers, at both the Central and state levels, to interfere in routine administrative matters and day-to-day implementation of schemes and programmes.

Civil servants, on their part, learnt the art of being in the good books of ministers by being pliable in decision-making and doing exactly what the ministers wanted. As a result, civil service neutrality, which is a necessary attribute of how permanent civil services should function, is the casualty.

Neutrality

The primary responsibility of permanent civil services is to serve the government the community has elected. This means that civil servants must provide the same standard of free, frank, impartial, and responsive advice, and the same level of professionalism in administration and delivery of services, policies, and programmes, irrespective of the political party in power. The civil services should be apolitical, performing its functions in an impartial and professional manner. This is the concept of political neutrality on which the civil services in India were founded.

Political neutrality is a cardinal tenet of the civil services. But, unfortunately, the vision of political neutrality no longer holds good. Changes in political governments, particularly at the state level have often led to wholesale transfer of civil servants. Political neutrality is no longer the accepted norm with many civil servants getting identified with particular political tendencies. There is a perception that civil servants have to cultivate and seek patronage from politicians for obtaining suitable positions even in the Government. As a result, in public perception, the civil services have been seen as getting increasingly politicized.

The increasing politicization of the civil services has serious implications for the principle of hierarchy on which the civil service structure is based. Most civil servants have now developed lateral links with ruling politicians, thus upsetting the hierarchical order. This affects discipline, but more than that, it makes civil servants look over their shoulder at their political mentors to see whether their actions would meet with the mentor's approval.

Advice in Policymaking

In a democracy, it is the politicians who set the visions and goals. Civil servants translate these visions and goals into effective policy priorities. So, we can define policymaking as the process by which civil servants translate the political visions and goals into schemes, programmes, and regulations. Governments cannot succeed in delivering the results that people want if the policies that are implemented are flawed or inadequate.

Giving policy advice to the political executive is the most important function of the civil service. It is the duty of senior civil servants to provide the factual basis, thorough analysis of all possible options and implications of any policy measure under consideration, and free and frank advice, without fear or favour, at the stage of policy formulation. If a policy being formulated is perceived by the civil servant to be against public interest, it is the responsibility of the civil servant to convince the political executive about the adverse implications of such a policy.

The higher civil services in India have always taken pride in their ability to advise ministers on sound policy. Now, questions are being asked about the performance of the civil services in this domain. Was the civil service's advice on the formulation of policies that could deliver what the government of the day wanted lacking in adequate evaluation of future consequences? Was the civil service more concerned with formulating policies that the minister of the day could get through the cabinet and present successfully to the press? Did the civil service go back later and evaluate

145

the results that were claimed at the time those policies were launched?

The tone of these questions suggests that the policymaking advice was not rendered professionally and impartially. In fact, overall policymaking in India has been oriented towards achieving short-term interests that would fetch votes. There has been a tendency to make populist policies without adequately analyzing their long-term costs and benefits. Civil servants working in policymaking have tended to support and recommend policies that the minister of the day wants.

It is true that policies in India are hastily conceived under political pressure and pushed through the legislature without adequate consideration of long-term costs and benefits. Some of these policies become liabilities and cause mischief for years before being abandoned. In India, the policies of centralized control of economic activities caused a great deal of economic and social hardship before they were sharply modified in the 1980s and 1990s.

Since our policymaking is heavily influenced by political compulsions, it is generally not based on evidence, research, or long-term planning. There has also been an unwillingness to make use of pilot schemes to encourage innovations and test whether they work. There have been few attempts to consult the users or involve them in the policymaking process. The process also does not take into account the direct or indirect impact of the policies on people. On the whole, the policymaking capacity of the civil services has been weak because policies have been made as a response to short-term, populist pressures.

Statutory Role of the Civil Servants

Civil servants are often in charge of enforcing laws. Some of them are required to discharge functions under various laws, which are almost judicial in nature. The role of the executive magistrate or district magistrate under the provisions of the Criminal Procedure Code and the Police Act, and the role of an assessing officer under the Income Tax Act are examples of these functions. In such cases, civil servants are required to act according to the law and principles of natural justice. When exercising discretion conferred by law, civil servants are expected to exercise it in their best judgement, and not at the instance of politicians.

There is now an increasing tendency on the part of the ministers and other influential politicians to interfere in the work of the civil servants in the exercise of such statutory functions. A civil servant who fulfils his/her functions as expected by the law, invariably finds himself/herself in conflict with ruling politicians. In the last forty years, the practice of ministers and ruling politicians trying to influence civil servants in the exercise of their statutory functions has become the rule, and not the exception. The civil servants who refuse to pay heed to such interference are often punished through transfers to unimportant posts.

Discharge of Delegated Functions

In a democracy, the power lies with the political executive, which is accountable to the people through the legislature. However, like in any large organization, the government has to function through a hierarchy of civil servants to carry out defined tasks at different levels and in different locations. This makes it necessary, in certain cases, for power to be delegated to civil servants at different levels of the government. Such delegation makes it possible for civil servants to carry out the day-to-day tasks of governance at those levels. Unfortunately, there is an increasing tendency on the part of the ministers and ruling politicians to interfere endlessly in the functioning of the civil services at all levels even when the power has been legally delegated to the officers. This has led to inefficiencies and poor service delivery.

Recruitment to the Civil Services

The Indian Constitution provides for autonomy and independence to be given to the Union Public Service Commission and State Public Service Commissions so that civil servants can be recruited through open, competitive examinations without any interference from the political executive. While the Union Public Service Commission has been in the position to develop a fair and transparent recruitment system without any interference from the political executive, the same cannot be said for the State Public Service Commissions. In fact, serious allegations of corruption and wrongdoings at the instance of the political executive have been made about the functioning of almost all the State Public Service Commissions.

In addition, recruitment is also carried out for a large number of other posts by the government departments and different organizations under their control at the level of both the Central and state governments. There are many complaints of irregularities taking place in such large-scale recruitment to the posts of police constables, teachers, bus-drivers, conductors, and so on, under the influence of the political executive.

Postings and Transfers of Civil Servants

Frequent transfer of civil servants is a big governance problem in India. This has affected governance because civil servants are not allowed to stay in a position long enough. The brief stay in a posting has made it difficult to hold the civil servant accountable for his/her performance. Even worse, such transfers have involved large-scale corruption.

Such postings and transfers of civil servants are done at the instance of the ministers and ruling politicians. Although there are very clear rules in every department indicating the level of officers who are authorized to order these transfers, it is the ruling politicians who order these transfers for financial considerations.

In most cases, civil servants approach the minister and the ruling politicians, and request for transfer to a particular post or position. Although there are very clear rules stating that civil servants should not bring political pressure to get transfers and postings, these rules are mostly broken, so that ruling politicians can provide necessary opportunities to selected servants to make money, and through them, have a share in the proceeds.

It is a fact that ruling politicians have made liberal use of the instrument of transfer of civil servants to make money for themselves. The picture is very clear at the field level. The local legislators (Members of the Legislative Assembly/Legislative Council/Parliament) have their choice of civil servants to be posted to important assignments in their constituencies. More often than not, these civil servants extract bribes from people who come to them for work, and pass on a sizable part of the money to the legislators and to their official and political superiors in the department. This is also true of other assignments in the government.

This process of transfer of civil servants is so lucrative that it has come to be known as the 'transfer industry'. As a former civil servant says,

Transfers of government functionaries have in many states, virtually assumed the status of an industry. Officials at all levels are repeatedly shifted from station to station in utter disregard of the tenure policies or any concern about the disruption of public services delivery and the adverse effect on the implementation of development programmes.

In Indian politics, it is commonplace to find that when a new government comes to power, it makes mass transfers of civil servants. Each change of government in a state, even when the political party in power continues to be the same, results in large-scale transfers. Such transfers can run into numbers often exceeding 30,000 at a time.

A lot of money changes hands when such large-scale transfers are made. At such times, the transfer industry resembles a wholesale market where lucrative posts are sold to the highest bidders. After a change of political government in Maharashtra in 1995, a minister stopped all ongoing transfers in his department on the ground that over Rs 10–15 crore had changed hands in these transactions. The minister even quoted the rates charged for the transfer of civil servants at various levels. This happens in the state governments all over the country and all the time. Arbitrary and motivated transfers of civil servants, not in public interest and good governance, have become a matter of great concern. The scenario is somewhat better at the level of the Central Government.

Questionable methods of appointments, promotions, and transfers of civil servants at the behest of the political executive have led to a deterioration of civil service values. Such practices have increased temptation for civil servants to collude with the political executive in committing crimes or unprofessional acts. In fact, this has been the main contributing factor to increasing corruption in the country.

9

Civil Service Reforms

Since independence, there have been more than 600 committees and commissions at the Central and state levels to look into issues of administrative reforms. But only a few of them have been directly concerned with the question of civil service reform. The following are some of the major recommendations of the committees and commissions on civil service reform.

Recruitment

The First Administrative Reforms Commission

The First Administrative Reforms Commission, which was set up in 1966, gave a report on personnel administration in 1970. The Commission recommended that recruitment to the IAS, IFS, and other non-technical Class I services should be made only through a single competitive examination. It also recommended that the upper age limit for taking the examination should be raised to twenty-six years (it was twenty-four years at that point of time). It also recommended a new procedure for appointment of members of the Union Public Service Commission and the state Public Service Commissions.

The Commission recommended that direct recruitment to Class II posts should be discontinued and these posts may be filled up by promotion from lower cadres. It suggested that a simple objective type test should be conducted for recruitment to clerical and other secretarial posts. The Commission recommended that recruitment boards should be set up for selection of clerical staff.

All these recommendations were accepted by the government and implemented.

D.S. Kothari Committee

This Committee was set up in 1976 to look at the recruitment policy and selection methods in the civil service. It recommended a major change in the examination system for recruitment. It suggested a two-stage examination process: a preliminary examination followed by a main examination. The recommendation of the Kothari Committee was accepted by the government and changes were made in the examination system.

P.C. Hota Committee

This Committee was set up in February 2004 to examine the whole gamut of civil service reform covering the All India Services and Central Services Group A, and make suitable recommendations. The Hota Committee made several recommendations. It suggested that the age for entrants to the higher civil services should be between twenty-one and twenty-four years with an age concession of five years for members of the Scheduled Castes/Scheduled Tribes and three years for members of the Other Backward Classes. The Committee also recommended that aptitude and leadership tests may be introduced for selection, and that officer trainees may be allowed a time of one month after commencement of training to exercise their option for services.

No action was taken on the recommendations of the Hota Committee.

The Second Administrative Reforms Commission

This Commission was set up in August 2005, and gave its report on personnel administration in 2008. It recommended that the Government of India should establish National Institutes of Public Administration to conduct bachelor's degree courses in public administration/governance/management. Select Central and other universities should also be assisted to offer graduate-level programmes in these subjects. Graduates of these special courses from the National Institutes of Public Administration and selected universities should be eligible for appearing in the civil service examination.

Regarding the age of entry and number of attempts, the Commission recommended that the permissible age for appearing in the civil service examination should be twenty-one to twenty-five years for general candidates, twenty-one to twenty-eight years for candidates from the Other Backward Classes, and twenty-one to twenty-nine years for candidates from Scheduled

Castes/Scheduled Tribes. The number of permissible attempts should be three, five, and six for general candidates, candidates from the Other Backward Classes, and candidates from the Scheduled Castes/Scheduled Tribes, respectively.

These recommendations of the Second Administrative Reforms Commission are under the consideration of the government.

Training

Gorwala Committee

A Committee under the chairmanship of A.D. Gorwala recommended in 1951 that in order to have suitable personnel to staff the civil service, it is essential to have proper recruitment and training, and an adequate organization and methods set-up. It also recommended induction training to equip a civil servant with the necessary knowledge and skills to perform his/her duties, followed by training at regular intervals to refresh the civil servant's knowledge, keep him/her in touch with new developments, and his/her mind active, supple, and receptive. The Committee also recommended the appointment of a director of training to closely monitor all aspects of training.

The recommendations of the Gorwala Committee were accepted and implemented.

The First Administrative Reforms Commission

The Commission pointed out that training should prepare the civil servant not only for performing his/her present job, but also for shouldering higher responsibilities and meeting new and complex challenges in the future. The Commission recommended that a national policy on training of civil servants should be formulated. It also recommended for certain changes to be made in the content of the Foundation Course conducted by the National Academy of Administration, Mussoorie.

The recommendations of the First Administrative Reforms Commission were accepted and implemented.

Yugandhar Committee

A Committee under the chairmanship of B.N. Yugandhar was constituted in 2003 to examine the efficacy of the in-service training of IAS officers. The Committee made several recommendations to further strengthen and improve this training of IAS. It pointed out the need for three mid-career training programmes in the twelfth, twentieth, and twenty-eighth years of service. According to the Committee, the training programme in the twelfth year should be for a minimum duration of eight weeks consisting of five weeks of academic content and three weeks study, training, and exposure visits to study the best practices in India and abroad. The training programme in the twentieth year should be of twelve weeks duration. The Committee suggested that mid-career training at these three stages would bring about a 'major shift' in the nature of work of the civil servant.

These recommendations of the Yugandhar Committee have now been implemented.

The Second Administrative Reforms Commission

The Commission recommended that every civil servant should undergo training at the induction stage and also periodically during his/her carer. Successful completion of these training courses should be a minimum necessary condition for confirmation in service and subsequent promotions. The Commission also recommended induction training for Group D staff before they are assigned duties.

The Commission recommended that the objective of mid-career training should be to develop domain knowledge and competence for the changing job profile of the civil servant. To achieve this objective, mid-career learning opportunities relevant to specific domains should be made available to civil servants.

The Commission suggested that the composition of management bodies of national training institutions and those at the state level should be broadened by inducting eminent experts. The management bodies should also be given adequate power to enable them to discharge their functions efficiently.

The Commission also recommended that a national institute of good governance should be established by upgrading one of the existing national/state institutes. This institute should be given the task of identifying, documenting, and disseminating best practices, and of conducting training programmes.

The recommendations of the Second Administrative Reforms Commission are being considered by the government.

Placement of Civil Servants

The First Administrative Reforms Commission

The Commission recommended that a separate Department of Personnel should be created for formulation of personnel policies for the All India Services and Central Services Group A, and staffing of middle-level positions in the Central Secretariat. The government accepted this recommendation and established a new Department of Personnel.

The Commission also set out a policy on domain expertise. It classified higher civil services posts into two categories: (a) posts in the field, and (b) posts at headquarters. According to the Commission, the field posts were held by members of the functional services that included not only the various engineering services but also services such as accounts and income tax. The Commission noted that the only service that was not functional but occupied most of the higher posts in the civil services was the IAS. The Commission recommended that the IAS should be converted into a functional service.

The Commission recommended that administration should be organized along functional lines and talents should be inducted into the administration from all sources. For organizing the administration along functional lines, the Commission recommended that the administration should be divided into eight broad areas of specialization. It also recommended a scheme of reforms to enable entry into middle and senior management levels in the Central Secretariat from all services. This was to be on the basis of knowledge and experience in respective areas of specialization.

The recommendations of the First Administrative Reforms Commission about domain expertise were not accepted by the government.

National Commission to Review the Working of the Constitution

The National Commission, in its 2002 report, suggested that placements, promotions, and transfers should be managed by autonomous personnel boards.

The National Commission suggested that the personnel boards should be set up by law so that they can function independently like the Union Public Service Commission.

The recommendation of the National Commission was not accepted by the government.

Surinder Nath Committee

A group was constituted under the chairmanship of Surinder Nath in 2003 to review the systems of promotion, empanelment, and placement of officers belonging to the All India Services and Central Services Group A. The Committee suggested that assigning domains to the civil servants should be a key step for their selection to posts. The Group suggested eleven domains to which civil servants should be assigned.

The recommendation of the Surinder Nath Committee is yet to be accepted by the government.

P.C. Hota Committee

The Hota Committee pointed out that the absence of fixed tenure of civil servants is one of the most important reasons for the poor implementation of government policies, lack of accountability of civil servants, and waste of public money. The Committee recommended that an officer of the higher civil services should be given fixed tenure of at least three years in his/her post.

The Hota Committee also suggested that domain assignments should be introduced for civil servants to encourage acquisition of skills, professional excellence, and career planning. It recommended that empanelment and posting of joint secretaries, additional secretaries, and secretaries should be carried out through domain assignment, competitive selection, and matching of available skills with the job requirements.

The recommendations of the Hota Committee are yet to be implemented.

The Second Administrative Reforms Commission

The Commission recommended the creation of a Central Civil Services Authority to deal with matters of assignment of domain to civil servants, preparing panels for posting of civil servants at the level of Joint Secretary and above, fixing tenures for senior posts, and deciding on posts at the higher level which could be advertised for lateral entry.

The Commission recommended that domains should be assigned by the Central Civil Services Authority to all officers belonging to the All India Services and the Central Civil Services Group A on completion of 13 years of service. The Central Civil Service Authority should fix tenure for all civil service positions and this decision of the Authority shall be binding on the government. State governments should take steps to constitute state Civil Service Authorities on the lines of the Central Civil Services Authority.

The Commission recommended that the present empanelment procedure for short-listing civil servants for postings at the level of Additional Secretary and Secretary in the Government of India should be replaced by a more transparent process. At this high level in the government, the Commission felt that it is necessary to ensure that the tasks assigned to a civil servant match his/her domain competence as well as aptitude or potential. The Commission also recommended that some of these positions for which induction of outside talent would be desirable should be filled up by eligible persons from outside the government after suitable talent search.

The recommendations of the Second Administrative Reforms Commission are being examined by the government.

Performance Management

The First Administrative Reforms Commission

The Commission recommended that the term 'performance record' should be used in place of 'confidential report'. It also suggested that at the end of the assessment year, the civil servant should furnish an account of the work done by him/her during the year. This account should be the basis of grading the civil servant. It also recommended that the grading in the performance report should consist of three categories: (a) fit for promotion out of turn, (b) fit for promotion, and (c) not yet fit for promotion. The Commission also recommended that adverse remarks should not be communicated to the civil servant. While most of the recommendations of the Commission were accepted, the one about not communicating the adverse remarks was not accepted by the government.

Surinder Nath Committee

The Committee recommended that performance appraisal should primarily be used for the overall development of a civil servant and his/her placement in an area where his/her abilities and potential can be used. The Committee suggested that the entire performance record including the overall grade should be disclosed to the civil servant and the comments of the civil servant on the assessment of his/her performance should be taken into consideration. The Committee also recommended that only those civil servants who have shown good performance and have the necessary knowledge and skills required for higher responsibilities should be promoted.

The recommendations of the Surinder Nath Committee were accepted by the government.

P.C. Hota Committee

The Committee recommended that the existing system of Annual Confidential Records should be replaced with a system of performance assessment. In the latter, greater emphasis is placed on objective assessment against agreed work plans.

The recommendation of the Hota Committee was accepted by the government.

The Second Administrative Reforms Commission

The Commission recommended that the existing performance appraisal system should be strengthened by making the appraisal more consultative and transparent, changing the format to be job-specific, and making the appraisal a year-round one. The Commission also recommended that the scope of the present system should be suitably expanded so as to make it a comprehensive management system. It suggested that an annual performance agreement should be signed between the departmental minister and the secretary of the department, providing physical and verifiable details of the work to be done during the year. The actual performance should be assessed by a third party, say, the Central Civil Services Authority, with reference to the performance agreement. The various recommendations of the Second Administrative

Reforms Commission are being considered by the government.

Accountability

The Committee on Prevention of Corruption

The Committee, known as the Santhanam Committee, recommended the creation of the Central Vigilance Commission, and vigilance divisions in all departments and major organizations of the government. It suggested that rules should be framed for governing the conduct of civil servants. The Committee further suggested that on completing 25 years of service or 50 years of age, a civil servant may be retired from service, if the government found him unfit to continue. These recommendations of the Santhanam Committee were accepted and implemented by the government.

The First Administrative Reforms Commission

The Commission recommended that all departments which are in direct charge of development programmes should introduce performance budgeting. It also recommended the establishment of two special institutions: The Lokpal to deal with complaints against administrative acts of the ministers and secretaries to the Government of India and Lokayuktas to deal with such complaints in the state governments.

The recommendations of the Commission were accepted. To start with, performance budgeting was introduced in selected departments, and later, in all departments of the Government of India. Laws were passed by many states to set up the institution of Lokayukta. The Government has been trying to pass the Lokpal Bill in the Parliament for a number of years.

P.C. Hota Committee

The Hota Committee recommended that a code of ethics be drawn up for civil servants incorporating the core values of integrity, merit, and excellence. Another recommendation was that each department should prescribe the services to be delivered by civil servants, and the methods of grievance redressal and public evaluation of performance. The Committee also recommended that a model code of governance should be drawn up, describing the standards of governance to be made available to citizens.

The recommendations of the Hota Committee are being considered by the government.

The Second Administrative Reforms Commission

The Commission recommended that a system of two intensive reviews—one after completing fourteen years of service, and another after completing twenty years of service—should be initiated for all civil servants. The first review after fourteen years should be for the purpose of informing the civil servant about his/her strengths and shortcomings for future progress in career. The second review after twenty years should be to assess the fitness of the civil servant for further continuation in service. The services of those civil servants who are found to be unfit should be discontinued.

The recommendations of the Second Administrative Reforms Commission are being considered by the government.

Relations between the Political Executive and Civil Servants

The Second Administrative Reforms Commission recommended that there is a need to safeguard the political neutrality and impartiality of the civil servants. According to the Commission, the onus lies equally with the political executive and the civil servants. The Commission recommended that this should be included in the Code of Ethics for ministers as well as in the Code of Conduct for civil servants.

The Commission emphasized that it is essential to lay down certain norms for recruitment to the government departments to avoid complaints of favouritism, nepotism, corruption, and abuse of power. The Commission suggested that these norms should cover (a) a well-defined procedure for recruitment to all government jobs, (b) wide publicity and open competition for recruitment to all posts, (c) reduction of secrecy in the recruitment process, (d) selection primarily on the basis of a written examination with minimum weight being given for interview.

These recommendations of the Second Administrative Reforms Commission are being considered by the government.

On the whole, there have been many committees and commissions which have made valuable suggestions for enhancing the quality of the civil service, but most of these suggestions are either being examined or have not been acted upon. The challenge of reforming our civil service is substantial and urgent. What we need to do now is to change our present civil service into a modern one that represents the best practices overseas, is committed to continuous improvement, and incorporates modern management philosophy and techniques.

Conclusion

The changes that India has experienced in its economic, political, and social structure since independence have affected the role of the civil services in many ways. The most dramatic change came with the new economic policy in 1991, which signalled the end of the licence raj, a rollback of the State in economic activities, and adoption of policies to create a favourable environment for private sector participation. It changed the role of the State from principal investor to facilitator of entre-preneurship. The new economic policy, which ushered in an impressive regime of deregulation, liberalization, and competition, meant considerable reduction in the discretionary powers of civil servants, and emphasized management of the economy through market-driven approaches. In other words, the civil services were now required to play a new role: That of being the facilitator of entrepreneurship. This meant new definitions of the professional obligations of civil servants, which are very different from the command and control methods traditionally used.

The new regime of deregulation, liberalization, and competition also asked for the involvement of the private sector and civil society organizations in the management of a variety of government activities. Increasingly, private sector organizations and NGOs were associated with public service delivery functions, which used to be managed by the civil services earlier. For the civil services, this meant transfer of functions, loss of expertise, and the breakdown of the traditional relationship of command and control. Civil servants were now asked to be facilitators; they had to create a favourable environment for the entry of players from the non-governmental sector for delivery of public service functions. It also meant that civil servants could no longer expect to give orders to these players from the non-governmental sectors, but had to accept them as partners.

The 73rd and 74th amendments to the Constitution also changed the role of the civil services in a significant way. These amendments transferred the exercise of financial and administrative power to the elected members of local bodies such as the *zilla*, intermediate, and *gram* panchayats in rural areas, and municipalities and corporations in urban areas. Prior to these amendments, the administration of these local bodies was in the hands of civil servants. With these amendments establishing a governance system in which locally elected representatives planned, managed, regulated, and monitored development programmes in the local bodies, the role of civil servants changed from that of implementers to facilitators.

On the whole, the roles of the civil services have diversified since the time the country became independent. It has been a mix of regulatory, developmental, and facilitative. The important question is: What has been the contribution of the civil service, in the discharge of its multiple roles, to the development of post-independence India? In its regulatory role, it has contributed enormously to stability in terms of preservation of order, maintenance of peace, conducting of fair elections, and sustaining the unity and integrity of the nation. The importance of this contribution cannot be overemphasized in a country that has been troubled, time and again, by regional and linguistic chauvinisms, demands for independence and greater autonomy from military elements in different parts of the country, religious fanaticism, communal divides, and ultra-left extremism. Moreover, India has remained a democracy for more than sixty years and has seen a number of peaceful transfers of power both at Central and state levels. The part played by the civil services in the preservation of democracy and peaceful transfers of power has been very constructive.

For development, the civil services have played a positive role. Starting with the first Five-Year Plan (1951–5) when development efforts were modest as they were limited to only a few Community Development projects consisting of elementary activities, these efforts have expanded greatly during subsequent Plan periods. During the second Five-Year Plan period, the civil services played a pioneering role in state-led industrialization, with the public sector poised to reach commanding heights. In the third Five-Year Plan period, the civil service had a lot to do with the development of agriculture through encouraging production of new seeds and fertilizers, stepping up of agricultural credit, accelerating rural electrification and promoting the Green Revolution.

During the next Plan periods, the contribution of the civil services was even more positive. It led the frontal attack on poverty by building an income-generating asset base for self-employment of the rural poor, by creating opportunities for wage employment through a number of wage employment programmes, and by implementing area development schemes in backward regions of the country. Even now, the civil services are active in the implementation of pro-poor programmes such as Sarva Shiksha Abhiyan, Mid-day Meals Scheme, Rajiv Gandhi Drinking Water Mission, Total Sanitation Campaign, National Rural Health Mission, Integrated Child Development Services, National Rural Employment Guarantee Scheme, and Jawaharlal Nehru National Urban Renewal Mission. These flagship social sector programmes account for at least 18 per cent of the Central Government's annual spending. The mega Food Security Bill, the implementation of which is expected to start next year, would increase the outlay even further.

The important question is: what has been the impact of these developmental schemes and programmes? It has brought about significant improvements in the lives of the people. The percentage of India's population below the poverty line has come down to 28 per cent. Indicators of human development such as literacy and education, and maternal and infant mortality rates have shown steady improvement. The literacy rate has gone up from 18.3 per cent in 1951 to 64.8 per cent in 2001. Life expectancy at birth has increased from approximately 32 years for both males and females in 1951 to 63.9 years for males and 66.9 years for females in 2001–6. During the last few years, the growth rate has averaged almost 9 per cent, and if this growth rate is sustained in the years ahead, it would have provided the basis for expanding incomes and employment, and also, the resources needed to finance programmes for social uplift.

The civil services' ability to enforce the laws, rules and procedures, and to tender policy advice without fear and favour, has declined over the years, to a point where a large number of civil servants now act at the behest of politicians in the performance of their tasks. Today, it is quite common for the decisions of civil servants, in awarding procurement contracts, enforcement of regulations, and transfers of personnel, to be made on the basis of what ruling politicians want. Such political interference occurs at all levels: at the levels of the Members of Legislative Assemblies and Members of Parliament, and Ministers of the Central and state governments. Often, ruling politicians tell a civil servant not to tender advice in the manner the officer would like to tender it. Such political interference has affected the performance of the civil services as an institution and led to considerable demoralization within. Now that scams are out in the open and the concerned people are getting punished, most civil servants are not inclined to make decisions even when due.

These scams, widely reported in the media, have brought to the fore the prevalence of widespread corruption in the ranks of the higher civil services and ruling politicians. It is, thus, important to have the institution of the Lokpal as an independent body to enquire into cases of corruption against public functionaries, with a mechanism for filing complaints and conducting enquiries. The first Administrative Reforms Commission, while recommending the creation of the institution of Lokpal, was of the view that the institution was necessary not only for removing the sense of injustice from the minds of the affected citizens but also for instilling public confidence in the efficiency of the administrative machinery.

The first Lokpal Bill was proposed and passed in Lok Sabha in 1969 but could not get through Rajya Sabha. Subsequently, Lokpal Bills were introduced in 1971, 1977, 1985, 1989, 1996, 1998, 2001, 2005, and 2008, and yet, were never passed. The Lokpal Bill 2011 was introduced in Parliament on 4 August 2011. The highlights of the 2011 Bill are: (a) it seeks to establish the office of the Lokpal to investigate and prosecute cases of corruption, (b) it covers the prime minister after he leaves office, ministers, Members of Parliament, Group A officers and officers of organizations which are either government-aided or funded by public donations, (c) any person may make a complaint against a public servant within seven years of the offence, and the Bill provides a process for investigation and enquiry, (d) if the Lokpal finds that an offence has been committed, it may recommend disciplinary action and file a case in the Special Court, (e) the Bill enhances penalties for certain offences under the Prevention of Corruption Act from seven years to ten years, and it also imposes penalties for false and frivolous complaints, and (f) all expenses of the Lokpal will be charged to the Consolidated Fund of India.

Lok Sabha passed the 2011 Lokpal Bill on 27 December 2011 with certain modifications. The Bill is yet to get acceptance from the Rajya Sabha and it has been deferred to the next parliamentary session. In any case, Anna Hazare, who fought for a bill on Lokpal to be passed in Parliament, has claimed that the Lokpal Bill passed by Lok Sabha on 27 December 2011 is weak and will not serve any purpose. Anna Hazare and his associates have proposed the adoption of a Jan Lokpal Bill, drafted by prominent civil society activists, seeking the creation of a Jan Lokpal, an independent body that would investigate corruption cases, complete the investigation within a year, and in case it goes to trial, complete it in the next one year. However, it is important that an independent Lokpal be set up by law to enquire into cases of corruption by public functionaries.

It is also necessary to enact a civil service law that would describe the core principles, values, and characteristics which create its culture and ethos. Such a law would also provide a clear and unified framework within which the civil services can carry out its responsibilities. It would also provide a legal basis for the legislature to express the important values and culture it wants in the civil services. In that case, the civil service law would become an unambiguous statement, to those within the civil services, and to the people of India, of what is expected of the bureaucracy.

Countries like Australia and New Zealand, which have reformed and modernized their civil services, have greatly benefited from the enactment of civil service laws. In these two countries, civil service laws—the Australian Public Service Act 1999 and the New Zealand State Sector Act, 1988—have provided the basis for civil service reform. The civil service laws both in Australia and New Zealand set out the directions for change and reform. They provide the required administrative and financial flexibility to civil servants. The employment framework was transformed in these countries, providing the civil services with the freedom necessary to achieve results. These laws also created the conditions for the emergence of a cohesive civil service welded together by shared values rather than by processes and regulations. In other words, the governments in these two countries were able to modernize their civil services to be compatible with the requirements of the twenty-first century.

Currently, a draft civil service bill is being prepared. However, widespread discussions on the draft bill are needed. This will achieve two important objectives. First, it will help incorporate issues and set doubts at rest. Second, it will also help in garnering general, wide-ranging support for the need to make changes in the formal framework of the civil services. These are key requirements for nations competing in the twenty-first century.

In India, we do not have a positive statement of values that can guide the conduct of civil servants. What we have instead is a set of rules, which lays down what civil servants should not do. What we need is a legal declaration of values and a code of conduct reflecting public expectations of the relationship between the civil services and the government, the legislature, and the members of the public, with specific reference to political impartiality, maintenance of the highest ethical standards, accountability for actions, and responsibilities to the government of the day.

Countries like the UK, Australia, and New Zealand have drawn up a legal declaration of values and codes for conduct for civil servants. In the UK, following the recommendations of the Nolan Committee on the standards in public service, the Civil Service Code was incorporated into a law that came into force on 1 January 1996. The Code is a clear and concise statement of the standards of behaviour that civil servants must follow, and is a part of civil servants' terms and conditions of employment.

In Australia, Section 10 of the Public Service Act, 1999 contains a declaration of 15 values for the members of the Australian Public Service. Section 13 of the Australian Act lays down the Code of Conduct for Australia's civil services. New Zealand has enacted the State Services Act that focuses on ethics and public service ethos. The State Services Commission in New Zealand has issued a Code of Conduct for civil servants. In India also, we should have a declaration of values and a code of conduct for civil servants, and preferably, make them a part of the civil service law.

In fact, our task now should be to build a civil service which India needs in the twenty-first century. We are already engaged in the task of building an inter-nationally competitive India which, through increased productivity, will allow Indians to enjoy improved standards of living, gainful employment, and better access to public services. A key to this transformation is to build modern civil services.

There is yet another compelling reason. Sweeping changes that are taking place in the global economy make it necessary for us to build competent civil services. In a globalized world, countries compete in the global marketplace, and the quality of administration is reflected in these battles. It has made it necessary for countries to improve their competitiveness across the board.

What should civil services for the twenty-first century India look like? It should be a civil service that is valued by ministers, and is an excellent source of expert, objective policy advice. It should be able to deliver world-class, customer-focused services, day-in and day-out, frequently in partnership. It should attract the best talents from every area of the society. The civil servants should be honest, objective, impartial, accountable, result-oriented, and transparent in their dealings. It should be a civil service in which officers are proud of, and passionate about their work, committed to doing what they have to do with the pace that India needs and expects in the twenty-first century, and with the right professional skills. Finally, the civil services should be such that every part of it commands the confidence and respect of the public it serves.

Further Reading

Administrative Reforms Commission. 1969. *Report on Personnel Administration*. New Delhi: Government of India.

Allen, C. (ed.). 1979. *Plain Tales from the Raj: Images of British India in the Twentieth Century*. London: Futura Publications.

Arora, R. and R. Goyal. 1995. *Indian Public Administration: Institutions and Issues*. Delhi: Wishwa Prakashan.

Das, S.K. 2010. *Building a World-Class Civil Service for Twenty-first Century India*. New Delhi: Oxford University Press.

Dewey, C. 1996. *The Mind of the Indian Civil Service*. New Delhi: Oxford University Press.

Krishnan, K.P. and T.V. Somanathan. 2005. 'Civil Service: An Institutional Perspective', in D. Kapur and P.B. Mehta (eds), *Public Institutions in India: Performance and Design*. New Delhi: Oxford University Press, pp. 258–319.

Macaulay Committee Report. 1975. *The Civil Service (Fulton Committee Report)*, Vol. 1. London: HMSO.

P.C. Hota Committee Report. 2004. *Civil Service Reform*. New Delhi: Government of India.

Potter, D.C. 1996. *India's Political Administrators: From ICS to IAS*. New Delhi: Oxford University Press.

Second Administrative Reforms Commission. 2008. *Refurbishing of Personnel Administration: Scaling New Heights*, Tenth Report. New Delhi: Government of India.

Surinder Nath Committee. 2003. *Report to Review the System of Performance Appraisal, Promotion, Empanelment and Placement*. New Delhi: Government of India.

Index

4·B·S
351794
27·1·14